THE DIVINE AND THE HUMAN

By the same Author

FREEDOM AND THE SPIRIT
THE DESTINY OF MAN
THE ORIGIN OF RUSSIAN COMMUNISM
THE MEANING OF HISTORY
SOLITUDE AND SOCIETY
SPIRIT AND REALITY
SLAVERY AND FREEDOM
THE RUSSIAN IDEA
TOWARDS A NEW EPOCH

NICOLAS BERDYAEV

THE DIVINE
AND
THE HUMAN

LONDON
GEOFFREY BLES
MCMXLIX

TRANSLATED FROM THE RUSSIAN BY R. M. FRENCH

Printed in Great Britain by
Robert MacLehose and Company Ltd
The University Press Glasgow
for Geoffrey Bles Ltd
52 Doughty Street London WC 1
First Published 1949

TO
LYDIA BERDYAEV

Preface

Max Stirner said, '*Ich habe meine Sache auf Nichts gestellt*,' 'I have based my case on Nothing.' I for my part say that I have based my case upon Freedom. Freedom is Nothing, in the sense that it is not one of the realities of the natural world, it is not a certain thing. So I have given my first chapter the ironic title: 'An undevout meditation.' Traditionally, devout meditation does not start from freedom. As a son of freedom I accept the free criticism of historical Christianity, and the free criticism of revelation, and it should be of the same kind as the criticism of pure reason.[1] This book is not about dogma, it is not in the least theological, though it might perhaps claim the right to say that it is 'believing'. Philosophy should be concerned not only with scientific knowledge but also with the religious way of life. 'Scientism' is a false and limited philosophy.

In this book it is my wish to give expression to the inward spiritual conflict which we have experienced in recent years, the torments and sufferings we have undergone, to our conquest of them, and to the hopes that have been ours. My thought, which is directed to that which belongs to the beginning and to that which belongs to the end, admits of only one possible metaphysic, and that is meta-history. Everything existential is history, dynamic force, destiny, man, the world, are history, God is history, a drama which is working itself out. The philosophy to which I would give expression, is a dramatic philosophy of destiny, of existence which is in time and passes over into eternity, of time which presses on to an end, an end which is not death but transfiguration. Everything, therefore, ought to be regarded from the point of view of the philosophy of history. And the philosophy

[1] This will be the subject of my new book, *Truth and Revelation*.

of history can itself be nothing but prophetic, and that which unriddles the secrets of the future.

I do not believe in the phenomenological method. It may be fruitful in psychology, it may be of assistance in metaphysical and meta-historical apprehension—but I believe only in a method which is existentially anthropocentric and spiritually religious—if indeed that can be called a method. Husserl wishes to investigate essences by the phenomenological method. Heidegger wants to investigate existences by the phenomenological method. But in that case the existences disappear, and objectivization results, which shuts its eyes to the mystery of the life of man, of the world and of God. Expressionism in philosophy is the only true path. The only possible metaphysic is a prophetic metaphysic, to use an expression of Jaspers's, and metaphysics in the grand style have always been such. Existential philosophy is the expression of my personal destiny, but my destiny ought to express also the destiny of the world and of man. This is not a transition from the individual to the common, but an intuitive disclosure of the universal in the individual. Philosophy, metaphysics, are not a reflection of objective realities, but a change within human existence, a revealing of the meaning of existence. Metaphysics is the *expression* of being. The world presents itself in different ways according to whether a man is occupied in commerce, in political conflict, in intellectual or artistic creativeness or in religious contemplation. And a man understands any particular thing only when thought is penetrated by feeling and the whole being of the man comes into action. That which is called 'being' is defined not by thought, not by knowledge nor idea, but by the whole subject, that is to say, by feeling, will and the whole bent. In this way various worlds are created. Truth is created in the subject; it is not given objectively from without. The world presents itself in different ways according to whether we are young or old, in good or ill health, happy or sad, learned or illiterate, believers or sceptics and so on.

It is impossible to approach existence; one can only go out from it. Truth is the act of freedom, it is created.

Kierkegaard says that truth is identical with subjectivity. God reveals Himself for the sake of the single person. God is present only in subjectivity. Objective truth is the death of existence. There is much truth in Kierkegaard's words, although it is not the whole truth and it is at times distorted. Jaspers says that the transcendent is to be captured only by plunging into the depth of the immanent, and this is what I also say, though I express it differently. Jaspers again maintains that the border-line position of man finds its support in transcendence. To him everything relative is objective, whereas the existential is in the absolute. In contrast to such existential philosophers as Heidegger and many others, I am convinced that religious experience, of the existence of which it is impossible to doubt, enriches knowledge and enlightens philosophy. But this presupposes a different relation between philosophy and religion from that which is commonly accepted. Present-day philosophy is hostile to the abstract. Its bent is towards the concrete. This was Hegel's objective also although he did not completely attain it. The dialectic of this book will be not of logic but of life, a living existential dialectic. It is characteristic of my thought to take an eschatological direction. This book will make it clear what that means. The book was written in an exceptionally difficult period of my life, both outwardly and within. This fact has its bearing upon the existentiality of the creative subject. It has required great spiritual concentration to avoid being overwhelmed by the conditions of life.

PARIS, CLAMART
1944–1945

Contents

CHAPTER I

An Undevout Meditation
The Crisis of Christianity
Critique of Revelation

There are two crises. The crisis of the non-Christian and anti-Christian world, and the crisis of the Christian world, the crisis within Christianity itself. The second of these crises is more profound than the first. Everything which happens in the world and which gives us the impression of something which is external and even crudely material, has its source in the inward and the spiritual. In a certain sense it may be said that Christianity, historical Christianity, is coming to an end, and that a rebirth is to be looked for only from a religion of the Holy Spirit which will bring Christianity itself to birth again, since it is the fulfilment of Christianity. The weakness of Christianity in the world, a world which is in the grip of movements which are the work of dynamic forces and often of demonic forces, is the weakness of historical Christianity, and points to a transition to eschatological Christianity which is concerned with a world of the future. Eschatological Christianity will also be the religion of the Spirit, a trinitarian religion which is a fulfilment of promises, hopes and expectations. We are, as it were, in an *entr'acte* and for that reason our epoch is a time of suffering.

The world is passing through a stage of God-forsakenness. It is difficult to understand the mystery of the God-forsakenness of the world and of man. We ought not to rationalize the mystery; and this very mysterious fact clashes with the traditional doctrine of the Providence of God. The crisis of Christian consciousness is profound. It reaches to the very idea of God and the understanding of revelation. Christians will have to learn a very great deal from those movements which appear to be anti-Christian and from atheism itself, for even in those movements one is bound to feel the breath of the Spirit. That which rises up in human consciousness against God in the name of man is also an uprising of the true God Himself. Revolt against God can only be in the name of God, for the sake of a higher idea of God. In a large measure the revolt against God and especially the moral revolt, presupposes the existence of God. In reality no atheists exist; there are only idolators. Atheism goes deep and suffers. It is not light-heartedly gay or full of grim hatred. It is an affirmation of God.

The God-forsakenness of the world is its burden. Franz Baader says the burden means that God is absent. And the world to-day is both heavily burdened and absolutely fluid. This load upon the world and this fluidity are connected with each other. There is nothing sadder than the fate of Christianity, the religion of deliverance and resurrection. The very idea of God and of divine Providence has entered into human experience in a distorted fashion. A servile idea of God has triumphed and in the place of God an idol has been worshipped. The relation between God and human freedom has been wrongly understood. The relations between Christianity and the realm of Caesar, between Church and State, have been realized in evil fashion. The legal interpretation of Christianity and redemption, which is so degrading both to God and to man, has triumphed and turned the religious life into a legal process. The reception of revelation has been determined by its human environment, which is subject to change and may improve or deteriorate.

Hitherto no critique of revelation has been written, such as might provide an analogy to Kant's *Critique of Pure and Practical*

Reason.[1] This critique of revelation should show what is the human contribution to revelation. There are two partners in revelation. It is divine-human. There is the one who reveals himself and there is the one to whom he is revealed. God cannot reveal Himself to a piece of stone or a tree; but no, even a stone or a tree reacts in an elementary way to the action of higher forces, and this is still more true of an animal. Revelation is tinged with various colours according to the state of the human mind and the whole trend and bent of the man. There is, as it were, an *a priori* element in regard to revelation. If there did not exist side by side with his baseness a nobility also in man, he would never have arrived at the idea of God and would have had no power to receive a revelation of Him. Not only the thought of man about God but revelation also is coloured by anthropomorphism and sociomorphism.

It is true that man creates God in his own image and likeness as sometimes he has created gods, but the really important thing is that this human image and likeness should approximate to the image and likeness which is divine. Here there is a mysterious dialectic of two, not the action of one from above in a downward direction. Man has made God in his own image and likeness, evil or good, cruel or merciful, a violent aggressor or a liberator, and so on. People, whole groups of people, whole nations, have adjusted Christianity, as they have all religions, to their own level, and have stamped upon the image of God their own desires, and applied to this image their own limitedness, and all this has provided an admirable opening for the denial of the very existence of God. What has been wrong with anthropomorphism is not that it ascribed to God the traits of humanity, or sympathy, or that it sees in Him a need for responsive love, but rather that it ascribes to Him traits of inhumanity, cruelty and love of power.

[1] I am engaged on a book, *Truth and Revelation*, a critical essay on revelation, in which these thoughts will be developed, as they cannot adequately be developed here.

In true humanity not only is the nature of man revealed but God Himself is revealed also. The social categories of dominance and power have been transferred to God and that was evil sociomorphism. But in truth God is not a master, nor is he a wielder of power. A wrong cosmomorphism transferred categories of power to God, but God is certainly not power in the natural sense of the word. God is truth and right. The worship of God as power is still idolatry. And God is not being, for that would mean the transference to God of a category of abstract thought. God is the non-being which is supra-being. God is the Existent but not being. God is Spirit but not being. Spirit is not being. The understanding of God as concretely existing Spirit is derived from profound spiritual experience and not from limited objectivized natural and social experience, which applies a wrong cosmocentrism and sociocentrism to the idea of God. It must always be remembered that in the sub-conscious stratum of every man, of contemporary man himself, the soul of his forebears dreams on, going back to the most primitive times. What then were the beliefs of that primitive soul above which only a few chosen ones rose?

The ancient soul was steeped in magic. It was by way of magic that it strove to defend itself against the elemental powers of nature which threatened it on all sides, a nature which was the dwelling place of spirits. Magic was the primitive technical skill of man. Primitive agricultural cults were magical in character. Magic sought to know the secrets of the spirits of nature in order to win power over them, in order to acquire the possibility of commanding the gods themselves. To know the name of any being means to have power over him. The rhythm of movement also is of a magical character; *Mana* is a magical power and upon it the social position of man depends. The magical element in religion is a quality which lies outside the moral sphere and only by a long-drawn-out process does the moralization of religion come to pass.[1] The material element has always been powerful in religions and it remains so to this day. The part played by the grains of corn in the Eleusinian Mysteries is well-known. It was a symbol of human existence.

Religious materialism which has had an enormous rôle to play even to the present time, is hostile to spirit and freedom. It is always a sign of the shackles of magic. Magic promises man power but it leaves him fettered to the cosmic cycle. The ancient beliefs of a world still pagan linger on even in the Christian world and distort the very idea of God; and this after Christianity has liberated man from the power of demons and of the spirits of nature. The ancient soul of our forebears believed that the gods stand in need of propitiatory sacrifices and sacrifices which feed them, that they need blood and human sacrifice. This remains in a different form in the belief that in order to propitiate the wrath of God human suffering is necessary.

The old slavery of man has announced itself in the legal interpretation of redemption, in the experience of the relation between God and man as a legal process. Aurobindo, an Indian philosopher now living, says that the conception of redemption fits in with slavery. The ancient Hebrew prophets rose above the religious thought which demanded sacrifice as the primary thing, and set truth and right in the human heart in a place high above everything else. But the prophetic element has never been the prevailing one in the history of Christianity, which has been accommodated to the average social level. It does great honour to Russian religious thought of the nineteenth century, that it always reacted negatively to the legal interpretation of Christianity. Human thought at a low level has interpreted Christianity as a very cruel religion. The element of cruelty in the interpretation of Christianity is to be found in Syrian asceticism, in the monasticism which is nourished upon the *Dobrotolyubie*, in Augustine, in official Roman Catholic doctrine, in Calvinism, in the doctrine of pre-

[1] See Raoul Allier, *Magie et Religion.*

destination, in the doctrine of hell. From the opponents of Christianity one might derive the impression that the coming of Christ had worsened the position of man.

The division into two races, the chosen and the doomed, is opposed to the spirit of the Gospel, which itself, by the way, has also been distorted by the human environment which received it. When man is a wild beast he imagines God as a wild beast also. When he is humane, then he imagines God as humane also. The inhuman idea of God is a relic of ancient darkness which calls for a protest from the new humanity. With a higher estimate of his own dignity and worth man cannot reconcile himself to a religion of fear, vengeance and hell, to the justification on religious grounds of cruelty in the world; and in this a process of purification of the knowledge of God has taken place. The transition to monotheism among the Hebrews was already an immense step forward, but the pure monotheism upon which Judaism set so high a value was still a monarchical despotic understanding of God. It is only the God Who reveals Himself in His Son, in the God-Man, Who ceases to be God the despotic monarch, and becomes the God of love and freedom, and this is a revelation of God in spirit and in truth. The divine Trinity marks the triumph over the monarchical ideas about God, which depicted Him as an oriental tyrant, and transferred to God the sociological ideas of lordship. But it is slowly, all too slowly, that the ancient servile beliefs are being overcome. It must be noted that in Indian religious philosophy the legal interpretation of the relation between man and God finds no place, but in that case this is connected with monism. The conception of God in Shankara is static. In Eckhardt, on the other hand, it is dynamic.[1] It is Christian dynamism.

The divine is understood either in terms of social images—master, tsar, father, or in terms of dynamic images—power, life,

[1] See Rudolf Otto, *West-Östliche Mystik*.

light, spirit, truth, fire. Only the second interpretation is worthy of God and worthy of man. Here too there ought still to happen an immense change in the knowledge of God, a change which will be an emancipating change. Man does not easily awaken from his ancient nightmares in which the ego has tyrannized over both himself and God; and hence the crucifixion of God. The ego has been a fatality both for the human self and for God.[1] It is impossible to insist strongly enough upon the fact that God is not a reality like the realities of the natural and social world. God is spirit. God is freedom and love. His final and definitive revelation of Himself is in a creative act of Spirit; in a creative act of Spirit God is realized. In a creative act of Spirit, in the creative act of knowing God and proving God, the birth of God takes place in vital fashion.

The old doctrine according to which God created man and the world, having in no respect any need of them and creating them only for His own glory, ought to be abandoned as a servile doctrine which deprives the life of man and the world of all meaning. God with man and the world is a greater thing than God without man and the world. Man and the world are an enrichment of the divine life. Amiel says that God is the great and uncomprehended Unknown. Léon Bloy says that God is the lonely and uncomprehended sufferer. They have understood God better than the theologians. Apophatic theology is always right as against kataphatic theology. It alone reverences the Divine Mystery and it by no means indicates agnosticism. In this lies the great truth of mysticism whose knowledge of communion with God is better than that of theology.[2]

All this leads to a radical transvaluation of the traditional doctrine of divine Providence, which has indeed led to atheism, for it

[1] This was once revealed to me in a dream.

[2] See R. Otto, *Das Heilige*. He has some interesting thoughts about the moralization, rationalization, and spiritualization of sacred things.

has made a theodicy impossible. God reveals Himself to the world and to man; He makes a revelation in Spirit but He does not govern the world in the sense in which the world understands government. The usual doctrine of Providence, which people reiterate in conventional words, without thinking out their real meaning, cannot be combined with the fact of the existence of evil and the suffering of the world. It is impossible to believe in the old doctrine of Providence, and of divine government in this phenomenal crushed enslaved world, which is subject to necessity, and in which it is even impossible to find an integrated cosmos.[1] They have told us that God is present in all things, but it is impossible to find the presence of God in the plague and in cholera, in murder and hatred and cruelty, in violence and evil and darkness. A false doctrine of Providence has led to an attitude of servile reverence before power and authority, to the apotheosis of success in this world and in the last resort to the justification of evil.

In opposition to this stands the tragic feeling for life. God is present in freedom and love, in truth and right and in beauty, and in the face of evil and wrong He is present not as judge and avenger but as appraisal and as conscience. And God is He to Whom it is possible to turn from the horrors, the abominations and cruelties of the world. There was much truth in the restless questioning of Marcion, although his answer to this question was mistaken. He did not understand the gradualness of revelation, and the break there is in it within its human environment, which is limited and cruel.[2]

Philosophically the transvaluation of the doctrine of Providence must be expressed in this way. The conceptions which have been worked out for the phenomenal world, and are applicable to it alone, are not transferable to God. Providence does not act in the totality of the phenomenal world, and it can be brought into evi-

[1] Contemporary physics have destroyed the old doctrine of the cosmos.
[2] See Harnock, *Marcion: Das Evangelium vom fremden Gott.*

dence only by means of terribly strained interpretations. In this world of ours is much which is irrational, unjust, meaningless. But there lies a great mystery in the fact that in the individual destiny of every man it is possible to see the hand of God, to see a meaning, even although it is not susceptible to rationalization. Not one hair shall fall from the head of a man without the will of God. This is true, not in the elementary sense but in a more profound sense, in spite of the fact that in the world, which 'lies in evil', it is impossible to see the providential government of God. This is connected with the interrelation of the individual and the common. Averroes thought just the opposite, that God is interested only in the general laws of the world and in the race, but not in the individual. He thought that if God knew the partial then there would be perpetual novelty in Him, which would contradict the petrified idea of God.

In this world of ours not only God acts; but fate, necessity, chance, also act. Fate continues to operate when the world abandons God or when God abandons the world. Moments and times of God-forsakenness are fateful in human life. Man and the world are subject to inevitable necessity as a result of falsely directed freedom. Chance on the other hand which plays an immense part in life is, as it were, a state in which man is lost and helpless in a multiple world, in which an enormous number of forces, which cannot be grasped and which do not lay themselves open to rational account, are operating. An unhappy chance which presents itself to us as entirely meaningless and cruel is an indication that we live in a fallen world in which there is no divine government as a whole. But this same unhappy chance may be given a higher meaning in my destiny, rooted as this is in the phenomenal world. The belief that everything which happens to me has a meaning, cannot be expressed in the cosmological system after the manner of theological rationalism. It must always be remembered that God is Spirit, not nature, not substance, not force, not power. God is

Spirit; that is to say freedom. God is Spirit, and that means that he must be thought of apophatically in relation to the realities of the natural and social world. The usual concept of Providence is derived from the government of a state. God is represented as if He were the autocratic head of a state. Emancipation from what remains of the ancient idolatry is what matters, and is of immense importance. Idolatry is a possibility not only in regard to idols but also in relation to God. Such emancipation is the purification of revelation from the base conceptions which the human mind has brought into it, and to set it free from servile religious ideas and beliefs.

Christianity teaches that the crucifixion of God was to the Jews a stumbling-block and to the Greeks foolishness. But human thought has distorted the great conception of the suffering and crucifixion of the Very God by introducing ideas derived from a fallen social world, and the relations which exist within it. Such are, for instance, the conception of the redeeming significance of blood, which is so degrading both to God and to man; that Christ suffered in our place for our sins; that God accepted the sacrifice of His Son in order to receive satisfaction for the sins of men, and so on. The Fall has been interpreted as disobedience. The absurd idea that God can be insulted has been brought forward. Redemption has been based upon the idea of *justitia vindicativa.*[1] Jean de Maistre says that man lives under an authority which has been provoked and the provocation may be mitigated only by sacrifice, that the innocent can pay for the guilty, that cleansing demands blood, that the suffering of the innocent is pleasing to God.[2] Opposed to this is the higher interpretation of redemption which is known as physical or mystical (St Athanasius the Great). A purified knowledge of God must recognize the mysteriousness,

[1] See Jean Rivière, *Le dogme de la Redemption.* He sets out all the theories of redemption.

[2] See Jean de Maistre, *Sur les délais de la Justice Divine.*

the incomprehensibility of the crucified God, that is of the God Who stands in need.

In totemistic cults the offering of sacrifice was the means of communion with the holy. The sacrifice of the victim, as it were, creates the holy. In this there was already a dim unenlightened presentiment of the mystery which would be seen in the sacrifice of Christ on the Cross. But even within Christianity the primitive pagan darkness has not yet been finally overcome. There is a paradox of religion and especially of the Christian religion: salvation is at the same time a threat of ruin. Christianity has been interpreted as a trap. Out of the fear of perdition was fashioned the chief instrument of religious government by man and by human society. To manifest a disinterested love for God seemed to Bossuet in his controversy with Fénélon to be a heresy. Theological utilitarianism has triumphed. Men have often thought that it was necessary to defend God, although in actual fact the need was to defend man.

A vigorous faith and an intense religious sense, have been expressed in history in two ways, either in the ardent pursuit of perfection and of love for the Kingdom of God, or, on the other hand in fanatical and cruel persecution of those who held other beliefs. To these two types there correspond also two ways of interpreting God. The final victory over darkness, and joy, are only possible given apophatic thinking about the divine; whereas the old way of looking at things, which has infected theological teaching, gives rise to gloomy thoughts. Purgatory, paradise, hell —all such conceptions still belong to this world. By way of checking our ideas about God, try to imagine that the Almighty God regarded the eternal suffering of His creatures as the highest good. Would it be possible to come to terms with such a conception? Nothing but a dreadful state of fear could make men become reconciled to Calvin's doctrine of predestination. A loftier and freer way of thought must recognize the humaneness of God. Otherwise that which is idolatrously called God is a devil and not God. God like man and the world as well, cannot be understood otherwise than in terms of value and value is creative activity.

There is a remarkable passage in Kierkegaard about a man's relation to Jesus Christ.[1] The call to those who labour and are heavy laden comes from the humilitated Christ, not from Christ in glory. But the Christian Church does not wish to recognize the kenotic Christ. Neither does it want to recognize the fact that Christ is a contemporary, a truth which Kierkegaard held particularly dear. Christ was in the world *incognito* and that was His *kenosis*. Therefore the acceptance of Him demands faith, that is, freedom. The immediate recognition of Him without any possibility of being led astray would have made the God-Man into an idol. Christ speaks only in humiliation and not in exaltation, whereas man wants to begin with exaltation and not with humiliation. To Kierkegaard the turning of the Church into an object of glory on earth was its ruin. Christ regarded suffering as triumph, and the necessary thing is to imitate Him, not to be enraptured by Him and to worship Him. I say further, that not only Jesus Christ but God also is in the world *incognito*, and the freedom of man is connected with this. Herein lies the mysteriousness of revelation, but men have desired to take away that mysteriousness and to make revelation a matter of necessity.

The reverse side of the denial of mystery and the divine *kenosis* has been atheism. It is not within man's power to deny the things that are visible, which pass judgment upon him, and he bows his head before their reality. But it is within his power, or he thinks that it is, to deny the reality of God. Man is given freedom to assay the denial of God, and that freedom is guaranteed by the *kenosis* and the *incognito* of God. Atheism means but an experiment in the life of man, a dialectical moment in the knowledge of God. To pass through the experience of atheism may be a purifi-

[1] See Kierkegaard, *L'École du Christianisme*.

cation of the human idea of God, and emancipation from a base sociomorphism. But there are two types of atheists, the atheist who suffers and the malicious atheist. I will not refer to the light-minded atheist. Dostoyevsky depicts atheists who suffer. Nietzsche was an atheist who suffered. But there are malicious and self-satisfied atheists who say, 'Thank God, there is no God.' Suffering atheism is a form of religious experience and even of piety. Malicious atheism commonly means that a man has not held out against the test imposed by the measureless suffering of the world and man. He is worse than the first type of atheist, but he too indicates above all a revolt against false and degrading ideas about God. Believers, therefore, ought not to look down upon atheists; they ought to enter into an experience and into trials which are other than their own; and this all the more in view of the fact that among believers faith has sometimes been too easily attained. Feuerbach was a devout atheist and through him the human conception of God has been purified. Man, society, and the world may pass through a state of God-forsakenness, and within the limits of human thought this may be reflected in the form of atheism. It is with difficulty that men bear the *incognito* of the Divine and the *kenosis* of Christ. They would like an imperial majesty of God and the God-man. Men first of all rationalize divine Providence and adapt it to their own level, and then they rise in revolt against their own false ideas and become atheists. In the first state they were no nearer to God than in the second.

In the case of revelation, which is fundamental in the religious life, the same thing has happened as with all manifestations of the Spirit; it has been objectivized.[1] The fact must be recognized that Christian revelation could not have played a social rôle and could not have become an impelling historical force unless it had been objectivized, that is to say, socialized and adapted to the level of the

[1] This will be dealt with in my book, *Creativity and Objectivization, an Essay in eschatological Metaphysics.*

masses. There is a contradiction from which there is no way out within the limits of the phenomenal world. Objectivization is a distortion of spirituality and at the same time objectivization is a necessity for the realization of the destinies of mankind and of the world, for movement towards the Kingdom of the Spirit! But on the way, the illusions and distortions of objectivization must be stripped off, there must be cleansing. And this is the mission of the prophetic side of religion and philosophy. Revelation cannot be interpreted in a spirit of naïve realism, as it almost always is interpreted in books on theology. Revelation does not fall from without upon the heads of men. It is by no means a disclosure of any reality in the world of things. A philosophical critique of revelation, which has not yet been made, will have to be above all a critique of that naïve realism, in the same way as Kant's critique of reason was a stripping off of the illusions of naïve realism. It ought to be essentially a final emancipation from the illusions of religious and metaphysical naturalism. The critique of revelation which has been going on in recent centuries, has in essence been the final triumph of naturalism and the denial of God, Spirit and religion. What I have in mind is rather a critique of revelation which must lead to the triumph of spirituality, to the liberation of spirit from naturalistic and materialist distortions. God is not an object. God is not a thing. God is Spirit. One cannot enter into communion with the mystery of the Spirit in any sort of objectivization. The mystery never reveals itself in the object. In the object only symbolism of the Spirit is possible, not its reality.

Revelation is the fact of the Spirit in me, in the subject; it is spiritual experience, spiritual life. The intellectualist interpretation of revelation which finds its expression in dogmatics is precisely its objectivization, its adjustment to the average level of normal thought. But the events of the Spirit described in Holy Scripture, the manifestations of the Spirit in the lives of the apostles and saints were not of an intellectual character, the entire spiritual nature of man came into operation in them. Thus the intellectualist rationalist doctrine of God as pure act, which has played such a part in Catholic scholasticism, is derived not from the Bible, nor from revelation but from Aristotle. That doctrine, professing to meet the needs of abstract reason, turns God, so to speak, into stone; it deprives Him of any interior life and of all dynamic force.[1] But God is life; life, not being, if by this term the rational concept of being is understood. Being is secondary, not primary; it comes to light after the division between subject and object; it is a product of thought, of rationalization. In this respect Indian religious philosophy attains greater heights and goes deeper than Western ontological philosophy which is too much subject to the categories of Aristotle.[2]

The only true path is the path of intuitive description of spiritual experience, and along that path it becomes clear that in revelation both God and man are active, that revelation has a divine-human character. The religious phenomenon has two sides; it is the disclosure of God in man and of man in God. The yearning of man for God comes to light in it and the yearning of God for man. Traditional rational theology denies this yearning of God for man from the fear of introducing affective passionate life into God. For the rational concept of perfection does not admit of yearning and need in the notion of completeness; it prefers the perfection of a stone. In that case the relations between God and man cease to be a drama of two which is capable of resolution in a third. Revelation is a creative act of the Spirit; it has both a theogonic and an anthropogonic character. It is only mysticism, which found another language, and Christian theosophy which have risen above the naïvely realistic interpretation of revelation, above the rational and naturalistic understanding of God. It was perhaps Jacob

[1] Franz Baader understood this admirably.

[2] See the most interesting of contemporary Indian philosophers Aurobindo, *L'Isha Upanshad, Le Bhagavad-gita*. See also a recently published book: O. Lacombe, *L'Absolu selon le Védanta*.

Boehme, the great mystic-theosophist, who was most successful in giving symbolic expression to the mystery of the divine life. Spiritual experience is expressible only in symbols, not in concepts. But a philosphical critic must understand this symbolic character of the language of religious metaphysics. The most important question in the critique of revelation, however, is a question not of metaphysics but of meta-history.

In the critique of revelation the problem of the relation of revelation to history is of immense importance. Christianity is the revelation of God in history, not in nature. The Bible tells the story of the revelation of God in history. The mystery of Christianity is bound up with the Incarnation of God. It is usual to say that Christian revelation is not a revelation of the Spirit in the abstract, but of the Spirit operative in history. God enters into history; meta-history enters into history. The coming of Jesus Christ is a historical phenomenon. It is a historical fact in time. But this fact gives rise to a particularly complex problem which has been made acute by biblical criticism, by the investigation of Christianity from the point of view of scientific history. Christianity took shape and crystalized when men trustfully accepted myths and legends as reality, when historical criticism and historical science did not yet exist. Can it be that my faith, upon which my salvation and eternal life depend, itself depends upon historical facts which are subject to dispute? Can my faith be preserved if historical enquiry, owing to the appearance of new facts and new material, proves scientifically that certain things which Holy Scripture relates as facts, had no existence, that they are not historical events but myths, legends, theological doctrines created by the believing Christian community? Official Church history does not recognize that such a problem arises, for it does not allow historical criticism to lay its touch upon sacred things. The way in which history has been falsified on this basis is well known. But spiritual religion is bound to acknowledge that no religion stands on a higher level than truth, for God is truth and is known in spirit and in truth.

This means that the concept of historical revelation involves a contradiction and is a product of religious materialism. It corresponds to stages of revelation which lie in the past, Only spiritual revelation exists, revelation in the Spirit, whereas historical revelation is the symbolization in the phenomenal historical world of events which take place in the noumenal historical world. But the whole mystery lies in the fact that the noumenal events break through and enter the phenomenal world. The meta-historical breaks through and enters the historical world. There is no absolute breach between these two spheres. But when meta-history enters into history, not only is it revealed in history but it is also adapted to the limitation of historical time and historical place. Light shines in the darkness. The infinite God speaks with a finite human tongue within the limited conditions of a certain period and a certain nation. Revelation is always concealment also; in revelation there is both the exoteric and the esoteric.

Scientific historical criticism ought to be absolutely free, for its work may have a purifying and liberating significance for Christian thought. But historical criticism cannot decide any sort of religious and spiritual question. It has its limits in principle. These limits may be seen in what is known as the mythological theory which denies the historical existence of Jesus.[1] The mythological theory, which is open to grave doubts on historical grounds, was even of some use, in revealing the limits of historical criticism.

What is called 'the problem of Jesus' is not soluble by historical investigation; it eludes its grasp. There are no adequate historical data for writing a biography of the man Jesus; and religiously

[1] Guignebert, *Le problème de Jésus*; M.Gognol, *Jésus de Nazareth*; Couchoud, *Le mystère de Jésus*; A. Drews, *Die Christus Mythe*; Batiffol, *Orphéus et l'Evangile*; A. Schmeitzer, *Geschichte der Leben-Jesu Forschung*; D. Strauss, *Leben Jesu*. This was a book of immense importance.

speaking that is how it ought to be.[1] It is a mystery which is not visible from without in history, but has been disclosed in the religious experience of the Christian community. The solution of 'the Problem of Jesus' lies in that sphere in which the historical comes into touch with the meta-historical. But for historical science the meta-historical exists not as a reality but as the beliefs and ideas of ecclesiastical societies. The error of the period which had as yet no knowledge of historical science and historical criticism lay in the fact that the historical was regarded as meta-historical, that is to say as sacred, and, therefore, elements of human origin and human distortions were considered an indefeasible part of divine revelation. This is especially clear in the Bible, in which the world of religion and phenomena of the religious order are to be seen, but very much mingled with that are ordinary historical events, and distortions due to the limited thought of the Hebrew people. The ancient Hebrew understanding of God was the product of the still unenlightened mind of the Hebrew people, and only in the prophets does an upward movement above this limited thought take place. Thus upon the Gospel also, in which the story of meta-historical events is told, there lies the stamp of the limitation in language and conception of the Hebrew people at a certain period of their existence. In it the eternal divine world only breaks through in flashes. The Bible, the Gospel, were composed as a matter of history, with all the limitation and complexity of the historical. But the supra-historical shines out in them.

There cannot be any historical authority, but it is owing to the fact that the meta-historical is rooted in history, that the historical receives a meaning. Christian revelation both acted in history and was distorted in history. In this lies the complexity of the relation between the divine and the human, the complexity of the inter-

[1] In this connection Guignebert's last book, *Le Christ*, is curious; there is a helplessness to be felt in it.

action of God, human freedom and necessity. The infinite revelation does show itself in the finite, but the finite can never find room for the infinite in itself. The vista of the infinite always remains, infinite creativity, infinite revelation. Man is not a static creature presented once for all in a ready-made aspect. Man is a dynamic creature, creative and developing. Infinity is hidden within him. The scope of human thought changes; it may expand and it may contract; it may become deeper and again be thrown up to the surface; and by this fact the gradualness of revelation and its incompleteness are determined. Infinity is possible in the revelation of the Spirit and the spiritual world. Crystalization of the finite distorts the view not only of the future but also of the past. Limited thought, restricted and superficial, the thought of the everyday man, of everyday life, receives the revelation which corresponds with its own nature. Objection can be raised to the possibility of a new revelation, a revelation which continues and becomes complete, only if one adopts a static view of man and allows him nothing more than an absolutely passive rôle in the reception of revelation. But revelation is divine-human.

Historicity has a positive meaning and a negative. Everything which exists, every living thing is historical and has a history. Historicity indicates the possibility of new things happening, and at the same time historicity indicates relativeness and limitation. Historicity distorts. Christianity is historical and therein lies its strength and its dynamism, and Christianity is distorted by historicity. It is distorted by historical time. It is made relative. Historism is in a deep-seated way a false philosophy of history, in fact historism actually makes impossible the philosophy of history, which always rises above the relativity of historism. Historism takes no account of meaning. Only messianic thought has construed the historical and makes possible the disclosure of the meaning of history. Messianic thought awaits a revelation in a future manifestation which proclaims a higher meaning to history, it awaits the appearance of Messiah and the messianic kingdom. Greek thought knew no messianic expectation; to it history was a cycle and the Golden Age was in the past, and, therefore, it had no philosophy of history and had no knowledge of a meaning in history. Messianism had ancient Hebrew and in part Persian-Iranian origins.[1]

Christianity remains messianic; it looks for the second coming of the Messiah and the messianic kingdom. But Roman Catholic theology opposes any introduction of the messianic idea into Christianity from fear of prophetism.[2] It is beyond dispute that primitive Christianity was constructed on an eschatological framework. But the prospect of a long historical road between the two appearances of Christ the Messiah was opened up; in the place of the Kingdom of God, the Church took shape, and Christianity, having become historical, began to adapt itself to this world, to the kingdom of Caesar. Only a few within 'historical Christianity' awaited the new revelation of the Holy Spirit and then frequently in a distorted form. The prophetical side of Christianity was weakened and disappeared almost entirely. Historical Christianity took on an organized dogmatic and authoritarian character. The historical Church was regarded as the coming of the Kingdom of God. The idea of the Kingdom of God with which the Gospel is permeated is a prophetic idea—'Thy Kingdom come.' There is still no Kingdom of God; our world is not like the Kingdom of God; it can only be thought of eschatologically.

The impotence of historical Christianity which is revealed in our time is determined and explained by the enfeeblement of the prophetic spirit, by a condition of ossification, and a spirit which is exclusively sacramental and sacerdotal. The expectation of a new revelation of the Holy Spirit has sunk out of sight. I shall say

[1] See the curious book, Autran, *Mitra, Zoroastre et la préhistoire aryenne du christianisme*.

[2] See a book by the Dominican Feret, *L'Apocalypse de St Jean. Vision Chrétienne de l'histoire*.

something about this in the last chapter of this book. At the moment the problem interests me simply from the point of view of a critique of revelation. One cannot repeat often enough that revelation is divine-human, that Christianity is the religion of God-manhood, that it assumes belief not only in God but also in man, and presupposes the activity not only of God but of man as well. Thus only can the tragic destiny of Christianity in history be understood. In the fine words of Franz Baader, man wanted to be man without God, but God did not want to be God without man, and therefore became Man. The idea of continuous revelation must not be confused with Lessing's rationalistic idea of the religious training of mankind. There exists a complex existential dialectic of the divine and human, and it is to be seen most distinctly in the German mind.

CHAPTER II

The Dialectic of the Divine and the Human in German Thought

The Significance of Nietzsche

The Dialectic of the Doctrine of the Trinity

The theme of God-humanity is the fundamental theme of Christianity. I should prefer to say not God-humanity, a favourite expression of Vladimir Solovëv, but rather God-manhood. Christianity is anthropocentric; it proclaims the liberation of man from the power of cosmic forces and spirits. It presupposes belief not only in God but also in man, and this distinguishes it from the abstract monotheism of Judaism and Islam, and from Brahmanism. It must be emphatically said that Christianity is not a monistic and monarchical religion; it is a religion of God-manhood and it is trinitarian. But the vital dialectic between the divine and the human has been so complex that the human has often been debased in the history of Christianity. In the destiny of God-manhood in history at one time the divine has swallowed up the human; at another the human has engulfed the divine. The very dogma of the divine humanity of Jesus Christ expressed the mystery of God-manhood, of the union of the two natures without confusion or identity. It was a symbolical expression of the mystery. But the monarchical and monistic tendency always existed in Christian history and sometimes it predominated.

In a former book of mine, *The Meaning of Creativity*, I said that to correspond with the Christological dogma there should be a new anthropology, a Christology of man. But that can only be completely disclosed in the future. There is still no real Christian anthropology. Among patristic writers St Gregory of Nyssa came nearest to it. He was the greatest philosopher among the doctors of the Church and he endeavoured to raise the dignity of man.[1] But he had few followers. Christianity alone teaches that God became man.[2] The gulf between God and man was bridged. The humanity of God was revealed, not only the divine in man but also the human in God. If the humility of Christ is thought out to the end it has to be recognized that the Second Person of the Holy Trinity is Man from all eternity, and this mystery by no means indicates an acknowledgment of the identity of man and God, which would be the equivalent of a drastically rational denial of the mystery.

During the first centuries of Christianity, when dogmatic controversies were carried on and dogmatic formulas worked out, in which men set themselves to express in symbols the events of the spiritual world, a complex dialectic of the relation of the divine and the human was developed. Both the rise of heresies and the condemnation of heresies were alike connected with this theme. Arianism, monophysism, monothelism, Nestorianism—all these were heresies concerned with the theme of God-manhood. The controversies were carried on in connection with the Christological problem, that is to say the problem of the relation between the two natures in Christ. But the real problem is broader and deeper; it broaches the subject of the relation between the divine and the human in general. Let it be granted that the Christological problem was solved in the first centuries and a formula expressing the relation of the divine and the human in Christ was found which lay beyond monism and dualism. But in our epoch—I speak of the epoch of the Spirit—the question presents

[1] See two new Catholic books on St Gregory of Nyssa: Hans von Balthasar, *Présence et Pensée. Essai sur la philosophie religieuse de Grégoire de Nysse*; Jean Daniélou, *Platonisme et théologie mystique. Essai sur la doctrine spirituelle de St Grégoire de Nysse.*

[2] In India the idea of divine incarnation has an entirely different meaning.

itself in another way. For the problem of man is posed with a keen urgency hitherto unknown. It is a problem which the patristic period did not know in such form, and thought about God itself is changing as an effect of the change in our thought about man.

The new soul has an awareness of freedom, of the quest for freedom, and the seductions and slavery arising out of it, of an acuteness and at a depth of which the Christian soul had previously no knowledge. The soul of man has not grown better, but it has developed and become much more complex, and to this fact a different thought corresponds.

Man has become less integrated, more divided in mind, and he has come face to face with new disquieting questions. The catechisms do not answer these questions. Men of the prophetic type have appeared in world culture, in literature and philosophy, men such as Dostoyevsky, Kierkegaard, Nietzsche, Vladimir Solovëv, Léon Bloy and others. The fathers and doctors of the Church, scholastic theologians have no reply to the subjects brought forward by such men. The prophetic fire has always been a regenerating force in a benumbed and chilled spiritual life; and another regenerating force has been mysticism.

Mysticism has a very close connection with the subject of the relation of the divine and the human. Mystics of a certain type have a tendency to monism, to the recognition of one nature only, to the extinction of human nature in the divine. All forms of quietism are of this kind. Jansenism is of interest in the dialectic of God-humanity. We meet with the classical pattern of mystical monism in the religious philosophy of India. Such is the religious philosophy of Shankara, who regards our soul, Brahman, the One, Sat, as the antithesis of any sort of happening and becoming.[1] The most remarkable among the present-day religious philosophers of India, Aurobindo, teaches that the idea that we are the

[1] See the book referred to above: Lacombe, *L'Absolu selon le Védanta.* Romanudja is opposed to Shankara.

authors of our actions must be rejected,—it is the universal which acts through our personality. Impersonality is the essential qualification for union with the divine. It is necessary to attain impersonality and apathy.[1] The soul is a particle of the divine.

Mysticism is often accused of an inclination towards pantheism, and on this account it is frequently mishandled. This is due to a failure to understand the language of the mystics. But it must be said that when pantheism is actually present, it is not so much a heresy about God as a heresy about man, a diminution of the significance of man, a diminishing of the rôle of human freedom and human creativeness. The evolution of European humanism, its inner drama, states an absolutely new religious theme; and that theme too is the theme of God-manhood.

The evolution of German mysticism and German philosophy is of enormous importance in the dialectic of the human and the divine. In German thought the category of fate (*Schicksal*) plays an immense part. This word is constantly used in German books on philosophy. There is nothing like it to be found in French and English books; and this is no matter of chance. The German people are a people of tragic destiny. This is linked with spiritual qualities inherent in that metaphysical people and with a sort of spiritual sickness in them. The notion that German thought and German mysticism are always inclined to pantheism and that the properties of the German spirit are of that kind has become widespread. Notwithstanding the undue extent to which this opinion has spread there is an element of truth in it which we will endeavour to make clear. I should say that the destiny of German thought is a drama in three acts and the whole drama is played out on the theme of the mutual relation of the divine and the human. Kroner, who wrote a most remarkable history of German idealistic philosophy says with enthusiasm that the metaphysical renaissance in Germany at the beginning of the nineteenth century was

[1] *Le Bhagavad-gita, interprété par Aurobindo.*

of a prophetic, messianic, and eschatological character,[1] and this is absolutely true. No such spiritual exaltation is to be found in French or in English philosophy. In France messianic and prophetic ideas were associated chiefly with social thought. The spiritual break-down of German thought is due to the extraordinary difficulty it finds in recognizing the mystery of God-manhood, the mystery of two-in-one, in which the union of two natures takes place without any confusion of them. But this indicates a difficulty in recognizing the mystery of personality. Anti-personalism is a property of all German idealistic metaphysics, with the exception of Kant who occupies a peculiar position. But we are bound to recognize that in German thought, in German spirituality, there has been a dialectic of genius which has had enormous importance for the destinies of European thought. How are we to describe the Acts of this great drama which is not only intellectual but spiritual too?

Act I. German mysticism and Luther. German mysticism means above all Meister Eckhardt. He is more complex than was previously supposed. He was not only a mystic but also a theologian, though he was greater as a mystic than as a theologian.[2] As a theologian he even comes near to Thomas Aquinas. But he interests me only as a mystic; he interests me when he speaks the language of mysticism and not the language of theology. In that lay his genius and his importance. And here in Eckhardt the mystic, there was an undoubted tendency towards mystical monism. It has been suggested that his teaching should be called not pantheism but theo-pantheism, but this makes very little difference. Eckhardt stands in the line of descent from neo-platonic mysticism; he shows kinship not only with Plato but also with Indian religious philosophy. This in no degree throws doubt upon Eckhardt's Christianity. I am quite sure that the religious philosophy of Thomas

[1] See Kroner, *Von Kant bis Hegel.*
[2] See a new book, A. Dempf, *Meister Eckhardt.*

Aquinas was not more Christian than the religious philosophy of Eckhardt, who in any case went down into the depths of spirituality in *Innerlichkeit*.

The most profound and the most original thing in Eckhardt is the idea of *Gottheit*, Deity, which opens up greater depths than the idea of God the Creator of the world, and lies outside the antithesis of subject and object. God is already secondary, not primary. *Gottheit* can only be thought of absolutely apophatically. The breakdown of Eckhardt did not lie in the fact that he asserted complete monism in regard to *Gottheit*. It lay in the fact that he affirmed monism in the relation between man and God, that is to say he was a monophysite. To him Creation was nothing; it lacked essential reality and value. Anything created is a mere nothing. The very existence of man is a sort of sin. Here the contradiction in German thought already comes to light. The great freedom of man in his movement inwards, towards spirituality, towards God is asserted, and at the same time the independence of human nature, the freedom of man, *human* freedom, is denied. A mystical determinism is affirmed. Rudolf Otto, who compared the mysticism of Shankara and Eckhardt, says that both are in search of salvation and of Being, and that to them knowledge is the way of salvation.[1] In Otto's opinion Eckhardt's mysticism does not belong to the gnostic theosophic type of mysticism, as Boehme's mysticism does. The distinction is truly grasped but it is exaggerated, for in Eckhardt there is a powerful metaphysical element which distinguishes it from Christian mysticism, which is occupied exclusively with a description of the spiritual path of the soul to God. German mysticism is always metaphysical and cosmological.

Luther is very important for the existential dialectic of the divine and the human. He had links with German mysticism though he himself cannot be called a mystic. Particular interest

[1] See the book quoted, R. Otto, *West-Östliche Mystik.*

attaches to his book *De servo arbitrio* which was directed against Erasmus. It is a very incisive book. There is a paradox in the fact that in the battle he fought for the freedom of the Christian against the power of authority over conscience, Luther absolutely denies the freedom of man and asserts the exclusive action of God and divine grace in the religious life. The one thing which must issue from man is faith; faith alone saves and faith also comes from grace; and this was in Luther's eyes emancipation from the power of authority. Man has no independent standing of any sort in relation to God. In relation to God there can be nothing but faith. But in such conditions man can be very active in the world. The traditional catholic doctrine of freedom of the will, on the other hand, and of good works which flow from it and are necessary for salvation, appeared to Luther as wellnigh a blasphemous mockery and an infringement of the almighty power and majesty of God. He not only denied the freedom of the will, but also regarded human reason as a devil. He accused Catholicism of Pelagianism. Luther's teaching about the slavery of the will has often been crudely interpreted and how profound and complex a metaphysical dialectic derives from him has certainly not been observed. It was difficult to foresee what German metaphysics of the beginning of the nineteenth century would inherit from this in the long run. The divine engulfs the human. This is an inward process in which the human is not subjected to force from without, but the mystery of God-humanity disappears as it disappears in Eckhardt.

The last and most interesting manifestation of Protestantism in Europe, the dialectic theology of Karl Barth and those who agree with his opinions, follows the same trend of denial of God-manhood. To Karl Barth God is everything, while man is nothing at all. And here we meet with a paradox in which everything turns into its opposite. Karl Barth is a dualist, not a monist. He affirms a breach between God and man, an abyss which divides man from God. But if man is nothing and God is everything and the one and only reality, this is another, concealed, form of monism and even of pantheism. If monism and pantheism are to be avoided, it is necessary that man should not be nothing, that there should be dignity and worth in man and that there should be freedom for him. Thus Calvin too was an extreme foe of pantheism, but paradoxically it can be said of him that he was a pantheist because he degrades man and lessens the reality of him, and because to him real being is God alone, and God is everything. So complex and involved is the dialectic of the divine and the human, so difficult it is to find a place for the mystery of God-manhood. This is revealed with genius in German philosophy of the nineteenth century. The only German thinker who came very near to the idea of God-manhood and divine-humanity and therefore came nearest to Russian religious philosophy, was Franz Baader.[1] But he stood apart from the main route upon which the dialectic of the divine and the human has been revealed.

Act II of the drama is German idealist philosophy, the most remarkable phenomenon in European philosophy. What is the link between Act II and Act I? The connection with Eckhardt was easy to understand, but the link with Luther is not to be grasped at once. The most profound influence upon German metaphysics was indisputably that of Jacob Boehme, but this is connected with another theme, not with the one which most interests me at the moment. The whole originality of German metaphysics, the difference between it and Greek and mediaeval metaphysics, the different understanding of the relation between the rational and the irrational are due to Boehme. But in the problem of the relation between the divine and the human in the problem of divine-humanity Boehme was much more of a Christian than Hegel or Fichte and less of a monist. It is very frequently said

[1] See a new and very thorough book on Franz Baader: E. Susine, *Franz von Baader et le romantisme mystique*, 2 vols.

that Luther was the father of philosophical idealism and that German philosophy blossomed on the soil of Protestantism.

At first sight nothing could be more contradictory than Luther and Hegel. The former cursed reason, as a devil; the second made a god of reason. To the former everything is due to grace and this is certainly not favourable to metaphysical knowledge. But if one looks at the matter from a deeper point of view, it is possible to understand why his repudiation of reason was turned into a bold affirmation of reason. Luther was not a philosopher; his was a prophetic nature and he could not reflect philosophically upon his malediction upon reason, nor did he desire to do so. But the reason of Luther is entirely different from the reason of Hegel. Luther's reason is human while Hegel's reason is divine, as is the reason of Fichte and all the idealists of the beginning of the nineteenth century. Hegel's reason, which is of the greatest interest in this connection, is not the reason of Luther but the grace of Luther. With Hegel it is not the human reason which apprehends, but the divine reason, and with him everything issues from grace. The act of knowing, a religious act, is accomplished not by the individual man but by the universal spirit. In the same way the ego in Fichte is not individual and not human, it is the divine, the universal ego. In German metaphysics of the beginning of the nineteenth century everything is on a razor edge and may be toppled over on to one or other of opposite sides. The philosophy of Hegel, which was its crowning manifestation, may be interpreted either as the final engulfing of the divine by the human and as an expression of the pride of man, or as the final engulfing of the human by the divine and as the denial of human personality. Both interpretations of Hegel are possible. The revolt of Dostoyevsky and Kierkegaard on behalf of the individual man was a revolt against Hegel, against his universal spirit, against the tyrannical domination of the universal over the individual. The expression that '*die Religion als Selbstbewusstsein Gottes*' belongs to Hegel.

E. Hartmann, who was inspired not only by Schopenhauer but also by Hegel, constructs his religion of the Spirit on this Hegelian interpretation of religion and the relation which exists between the divine and the human.[1] German metaphysics creates the actual myth, which can be made to serve both optimism and pessimism. Hartmann interprets it pessimistically. An unconscious God in an outburst of mad will created the pain of being. But in man the primordial unconscious God arrives at consciousness and the possibility of liberation from the suffering of being is revealed.[2] But in the optimist Hegel also God arrives at consciousness in man and this consciousness attains its summit in the philosophy of Hegel himself.[3] Thus was accomplished the deformation of the theme enunciated by the greatest mystical genius of the gnostic type, Jacob Boehme. According to the latter, who was permeated by Christianity and the Bible, out of the *Ungrund*, which preceded the being of the world, in eternity and not in time there takes place the birth of God and the Holy Trinity is unfolded, and the Holy Trinity creates the world.[4] In German metaphysics, which was full of themes of the old mysticism, the ideal succession is altered. Out of the *Ungrund*, out of the depth of the dark unconscious, the world is created, and in this world God is formed. Fichte, Hegel and in part Schelling teach the becoming of God. The world process is the becoming of God; in man God finally becomes conscious. Both a deification of man and a repudiation of man take place. There is nothing which is purely human, distinguished from the divine and standing before God in a drama which is being played out. The results of this become clear in

[1] See Eduard von Hartmann, *Die Religion des Geistes.*

[2] This is very well expressed by a pupil of E. Hartmann's: Dreuss, *Die Religion als Selbstbewusstsein Gottes.*

[3] On the interpretation of religion, see Hegel, *Vorlesungen über die Philosophie der Religion.*

[4] See N. Berdyaev, 'Studies in Jacob Boehme. Essay No. 1. The doctrine of the *Ungrund* and freedom.'

Act III. The principal deficiency of German metaphysics, that exhibition of human thought stamped with the mark of genius, was its anti-personalism.

The philosophy of Hegel which strove after the concrete but did not attain it and which crushed human individuality, evoked a reaction of the human against the universal Spirit. The divine was interpreted as an expression of the enslavement of man.

The third act of the drama began with Feuerbach, a very remarkable thinker.[1] According to Feuerbach man has created a God for himself in his own image and likeness, and alienated into the transcendent sphere his own highest nature. Man's alienated nature ought to be restored to him. Belief in God is an outcome of the weakness and poverty of man. If man is strong and rich he will have no need of God. The secret of religion is anthropological. The idea of God is replaced by the idea of man; theology passes into anthropology. According to Hegel God arrives at self-consciousness in man. According to Feuerbach the self-consciousness of man is enough. The self-consciousness of God in man is merely the self-consciousness of man himself, of his own human nature. In the one case and in the other there is but one nature. The absolutely divine is replaced by the absolutely human. Feuerbach proclaims the religion of humanity. The book which Feuerbach, the materialist, wrote on the nature of Christianity is written in the style of books on mysticism. Feuerbach's own nature remains religious. But the deification of the human is with him the deification of the race, of society, not of the individual man and not of personality. In this sense his philosophy no less than Hegel's, remains a philosophy of the general, of the racial, of the universal. He was not a personalist. This was the transition from Hegel and Feuerbach to Marx. Feuerbach marks an important dia-

[1] Feuerbach's chief book, *Das Wesen des Christenthums*, has been unjustifiably forgotten; it is as a matter of fact one of the most remarkable books of the nineteenth century.

lectic moment in the relation between the divine and the human in German thought; the thought remained monistic in its tendency; there was no God-manhood in it. Hegel renders to God what belongs to man whilst Feuerbach renders to man what belongs to God. Both of them jumbled up the divine and the human and the transition from one to the other was not so difficult. Khomyakov already foresaw that Hegel would beget materialism. Feuerbach was the child of Hegel, as was Marx later on. Thus did destiny overthrow that dialectic of genius.

The final step was taken by Max Stirner and in the end by Marx in one direction and by Nietzsche in another. Max Stirner tries to be more consistent than Feuerbach. He denies the reality of man, of society and other forms of community. To him the only real thing is one's own ego, the unique one, and the whole world is simply its property. His book, *The Unique and its Property*, sometimes reminds one of the old German books on mysticism in the same way as Feuerbach's *The Nature of Christianity* does. But this is the astonishing thing. It might be expected that Max Stirner would be an extreme individualist and that to him the highest value would be the individually unique. Nothing of the kind. In actual fact he is the same sort of anti-personalist as Hegel. It is absolutely clear that the Unique of Max Stirner is not the single man, not the human person, but a pseudonym of the divine. Max Stirner, like Feuerbach, conveys the impression of being a materialist. But on deeper investigation the Unique has an almost mystical character, and in the book about the Unique there are to be heard the tones of the old German mysticism in which the whole dialectic process of thought was conceived. The Unique is the universal, not even a microcosm, but the macrocosm. There is a certain element of truth in the desire that man should be master of the whole world, but Stirner's philosophy was powerless to establish this.

In Karl Marx the divine-universal and the general appear in

another form, as the social collective, as the perfect society of the future, in which also human personality may founder, as it foundered in Hegel's absolute spirit and in Stirner's Unique. Marx's origins were humanist.[1] He made his attack upon capitalism because the alienation of human nature takes place in capitalism, dehumanizing occurs and the workman is turned into a thing (*Verdinglichung*); and he wants to restore to the workman his alienated nature. This was a notable idea, and it was an extension into the social sphere of the thought of Hegel and Feuerbach about alienation. It is what I call objectivization. But in Marx there is revealed one of the limits of dialectic humanism, in which he passes over into anti-humanism. This process has a profound metaphysical basis. When the human is affirmed as the unique and the highest, and the divine is denied, the human in turn begins to be denied and to be subjected to the common, whether to the Unique of Stirner, or to the social collective of Marx. Anti-personalism always triumphs. This is revealed in another way, but with the greatest acuteness and genius in Nietzsche, and in his tragic destiny. Nietzsche demands special attention. Before passing on to Nietzsche I will note that Kierkegaard who although not a German was associated with German thought and German romanticism, experienced the same difficulty in affirming God-manhood, that is to say, the two natures. He would seem to deny the human nature of Christ.

The life of Nietzsche was the life of a sick and feeble *privat docent*, in retirement among the mountains of Switzerland; a lonely life without any occupation except the writing of books. And at the same time the history of the whole world was throbbing in him, and the destiny of man was realized by him more than by men of action. Nietzsche writes of the last things and of final destinies. It might be possible to define the fundamental theme of

[1] See a particularly interesting essay in 'Nachlass', *Philosophie und Nazionalökonomie*.

the life and creative work of Nietzsche thus: How is the divine to be experienced when there is no God? How is ecstasy to be experienced when the world and man are so base? How is one to reach the summit of the mountain when the world is so flat? Nietzsche was tormented by a problem which was religious and metaphysical in character. The theme of Nietzsche was above all of a musical nature and in this he was a typical German. But there was an astounding lack of correspondence between his philosophy and the depth of his problem. It was a biological philosophy, *Lebensphilosophie* rather than *Existenzphilosophie*, and it was linked with Darwinism and evolutionism. The eschatological idea of the superman was based upon biological selection. In Russia Nietzsche was always understood in a different way from the way he was interpreted in the West. To us he was above all a philosopher of culture.

The whole creative work of Nietzsche is occupied by three problems; the relation between the human and the divine, which to him is the super-human; the creative power of man, which ought to create new values; and suffering, the heroic power of holding out against suffering. The aspiration of Nietzsche towards the divine heights was expressed in the will to rise above man. He preaches the superman which is for him a pseudonym of the divine. Here the dialectic of the divine and the human is worked out to its limit. Nietzsche was the child of European humanism, bone of its bone and flesh of its flesh. But he arrives at the repudiation of man. Nietzsche betrays man. To him man is a shame and a disgrace, a mere transition to the new race of the superman. Zarathustra says: '*Eine dieser Krankheiten heisst zum Beispiel—Mensch,*' and again, '*Der Ubermensch liegt mir am Herzen, der ist mein Erstes und Einziges, und nicht der Mensch. Was ich lieben kann am Menschen, das ist, dass er Ubergang ist und ein Untergang.*'

Both the human and the divine disappear in the superman. The preacher of the superman enthusiastically acclaims Napoleon, on the ground that he is composed of the non-human and the super-human, that there is nothing human in him. Nietzsche has no use for man and the human. He would take his stand under the banner of fate (*amor fati*), and he did not desire the victory of man over fate, as Marx desired it. In this he found the tragic sense of life; hence his animosity against Socrates, his idealization of the instincts, his mysticism of blood, which is akin to that of Gobineau. He is a defender of the principle of heredity and of aristocracy. He is considered an individualist, but he was an anti-personalist. He does not notice that Dionysism is democratic, not aristocratic.[1] Antagonistic as he was to Christianity, which he knew only in a decadent bourgeois form which had lost all its heroism, he did all the same understand something about it. He understood that Christianity is a revolution directed against the aristocratic principle of ancient civilization—'the last shall be first'. With Nietzsche as with all German thought before him, there are not two natures; there is no meeting; there is no mystery of God-manhood. There is only one nature all in all. He is regarded as an atheist. This is an over-simplification, it is a failure to understand that thought and conscious ideas do not exhaust the depth of a man. It was with bitterness and suffering that Nietzsche said that God has been killed. There is an immense difference between the atheism of Feuerbach and the atheism of Nietzsche. Nietzsche would like God to return. Zarathustra said:

O komme zurück
Mein unbekanter Gott, mein Schmerz
Mein letztes Glück.

God torments him as He torments the heroes of Dostoyevsky. He comes near to the theme of Kirilov. His quest was for the super-man; but what must be sought for is man who is fully man

[1] Such a notable specialist in the religion of Dionysus as Vyacheslav Ivanov always said this.

'resent-day man is still not fully man; he is still half-beast and not ıfrequently worse than a beast. There is a deep-seated contra-iction in Nietzsche's attitude to man. To him man is a shame and disgrace. He will have none of man; he looks upon him as a ıeans. Yet at the same time he endows man with a capacity for reation, for the creation of values, the creation of a new world, nd with a capacity for heroic endurance of suffering.

The greatest service which Nietzsche rendered was his state-ıent of the problem of creativeness, He sought for ecstasy and or him ecstasy was connected with creativeness. He was convinced hat man can create new values. In his view truth is created and ot revealed. Truth is not a datum and is not received passively y man. It is created in a vital process in the struggle for power. nd life is a creative process in which all values are created. In my wn terminology it may be said that what is known as objective ruth is an illusion of objectivism. And Nietzsche was right in his hirst for creativeness, in his belief in creativeness. And indeed rom that Christian point of view which was so alien to him, truth the way and the life, not a thing, not a reality in the sphere of hings. Man is able to create new values, he can create a new life. 3ut there are limits to human creative power. A man cannot create ving beings; he can only beget them; he cannot create even a ea and there is a profound meaning in this. A creature created y man would have no living image; it would be a mechanism.

The breakdown in Nietzsche arises from the fact that he wanted nan to create superman, he wanted the divine, which was as yet on-existent, to be created by man, he wanted the lower to beget he higher. But from what source within himself is such a mere othing as man—and Nietzsche considered man a mere nothing —to find power to create the superhumanly divine? In order to ustify the creativity of man, his creation of new values, a new nthropology is needed.[1] But Nietzsche's own philosophy on

[1] See my book, *The Meaning of Creativity, an Essay on the Justification of Man.*

which he based his anthropology was old. It could see no creative power in man. Man, the mere nothing of a creature, is to create God. The dialectic of the divine and the human leads to the denial both of the divine and the human and to their disappearance in the phantom of the titanic super-human. The disease from which he suffered is given as an explanation of Nietzsche's madness, but it ought to be seen also, from the spiritual point of view, as the result of an inhuman overstrained effort to rise to dizzy height when at the same time there are no heights. It was an instance of that aspiration towards a heroic nothing which is characteristic of the German spirit.

Such was Nietzsche's stupendous vision of a dionysian world. Two ideas possess him—the idea of the eternal return and the idea of the superman. These two ideas are inconsistent with each other. The idea of the eternal return is the ancient Greek idea of cyclic movement. The idea of the superman is a messinaic idea and like every messianic idea has Persian-Jewish-Christian sources. It is not by chance that Nietzsche took the name in the title of the greatest production of his genius from the Persians, who brought the eschatological idea into religious thought. I attach little importance to the gloomy idea of the eternal return, but the idea of the superman is immensely important. In Nietzsche orientation to the future and to the past were combined, Prometheus and Epimetheus. There were combined in him both revolutionary and reactionary elements of the spirit. He was a victim of the denial of human creativeness by historical Christianity.

The other problem raised by Nietzsche is the problem of suffering. He himself suffered a great deal; he suffered from hopeless disease and from hopeless loneliness. He waged a heroic fight against suffering. No pain prevented his creative work. The power to hold out against suffering was to him the measure of the value of man. He desired to bear suffering with no consolation at all. He rebelled against Christianity because it would give meaning to suffering and in so doing provide consolation. It was only the endurance of suffering without any consolation, without any hope of another life that he considered heroic, and with him this was connected with a tragic feeling for life. He sought out danger; he loved to walk on the edge of the abyss; he wanted no guarantee of life.[1] How is Nietzsche's attitude to Christianity to be understood in its deepest sense? He was an enemy of Christianity; he regarded himself as its most terrible foe. He wrote about Christianity in very ugly and unjust terms. He wrote *Antichrist*, probably the weakest of all his works. But at the same time Nietzsche was a man who felt the wounding touch of Christ and the Christian theme. Anti-eros was linked with eros. He fought against Christ but he fought as a man to whom Christ was dear in the very depth of his being. When he was already in a state of madness he signed his letters 'The wounded one'. There is undoubtedly a strong Christian element in him although it is distorted.

Nietzsche, the foe, is much nearer to Christianity than Goethe, the well-disposed, whom the Christian theme left absolutely untouched. Goethe was indifferent to it. He is perhaps the one man of the Christian period of history who passed by Christianity and suffered nothing from it. He could arrange his interior life without Christianity. For that reason he is sometimes called the great pagan. But in Greece too he was unaware of the tragic religion of Dionysus. It is well known that Goethe had a great fear of suffering and strove to escape it; nor was he fond of tragedy. Kleist repelled him and he was very unjust to him. Sometimes his attitude to suffering conveyed the impression of cowardice although he was a strong man. On the other hand one cannot imagine Nietzsche outside the Christian period of history, however much he may have turned his attention to ancient Greece.

[1] There is a link between this and the contemporary French movement which is represented by Battaille, *L'expérience intérieure*, Camus and others. L. Shestov also had some influence upon this movement

His lot is the lot of a European in the Christian world. It is one of the paths that Christian man follows, a summit of his existential dialectic.

The case of Nietzsche is essentially connected with the dialectic of the divine and the human. This theme had already been set forth in the old German mysticism. In Eckhardt and in Angelus Silesius the very existence of God Himself depends upon man. This was always very disturbing to the theologians, who sought to find an intellectual and ontological meaning in it, that is to say a heretical meaning, whereas it was an expression of spiritual experience. When the mystics said that God depends on man, the statement can be interpreted in two ways, either it is recognized that two natures exist which meet in love and are found in interaction, or that one nature exists, for some only a divine nature, for others only a human. The path of German metaphysics led in the last resort to Nietzsche, with whom the human which he created means the disappearance of God and man. The significance of Nietzsche is immense. In him the inward dialectic of humanism reaches its completion. His appearance leads to the possibility and the necessity of a new revelation concerning man and the human, to complete the dialectic of the divine and the human.

Kierkegaard proposes that a start be made not from doubt but from hopelessness. Hopelessness to him is the distance between the subjective and the objective. But in the experience of hopelessness truth should be revealed. The inward cannot be completely expressed in the outward. To me this means that spirit, which is always hidden in the subjective, cannot express itself in objectivization; in objecitvization it is distorted. Kierkegaard is one of the sources of existential philosophy. This is apparent from the fact that according to him man and his existence cannot be an object. Existential philosophy is connected with religious unrest, and in Kierkegaard himself, it is determined by Christian experience. Men and their general view of life differ from one another radically according to whether they recognize the existence of 'the other world' or only of 'this world'. Kierkegaard's own experience was Christian, but it was the experience of a religious nature which moved forward through division, through the rupture of God-manhood, through God-forsakenness.

In Heidegger, the most vigorous of modern 'existential' philosophers, we see already a different state of affairs. Kierkegaard had some influence upon his problems, but with him God is replaced by the world, and hopelessness does not break through to something different. He wishes to construct an ontology, and to construct it by the same method and in the same way as rational academic philosophy constructs it. This is a radical contradiction of exisential philosophy, which does not admit the possibility of ontology, the latter being always based upon objectivization and rationalization.[1] Heidegger passed through the school of Catholic theology and this makes itself felt in his teaching about the Fall, the *Geworfenheit* of the *Dasein*. But the breach between human existence (*Dasein*) and the divine, reaches its extreme expression in him. *Dasein* is only *in-der-Welt-sein*. Nothingness is the basis of *Dasein*. It is a philosophy of nothingness. *Dasein* replaces the subject. With him as with Sartre, phenomenon, that which discloses itself, has a different meaning from that which it has in Kant. To-be-in-the-world is anxiety, being indeed is anxiety. Hence arises the sense of time. Heidegger's thought is oppressed by the object world of anxiety. With him there is no spirit, no freedom, no personality. *Das Man* is dull prosiness, and the subject of an every-day existence from which in actual fact there is no egress. His metaphysics is the embedding of human existence in the chaos of crude existence.

Heidegger's philosophy belongs to an altogether different epoch

[1] See M. Heidegger, *Sein und Zeit*, and the excellent book, Waelhens, *La philosophie de Martin Heidegger*. See also Sartre, *L'être et le néant*. Sartre decisively rejects 'the other world' and his philosophy is sheltered by such terminology as 'ontology', 'transcendent', which leads to misapprehension.

from that of the positivists, materialists and atheists of the nineteenth century. We find original sin in him, a legacy from Catholicism. With him the existence of man and the world is *Verfallen*, fallen. But whence did the Fall come to pass? Where are we to look for the blame for it? There are such things as moral values in disguise. As a legacy from idealism there is this, that truth is not correspondence with an object, that man communicates truth to the knowable world. But there is no justification of the possibility of knowledge. At the same time *Dasein* is historical being. History reveals the universal in the one. The creation of the future is the projection of death. Heidegger speaks of *Freiheit zum Tode*. The aim of our existence is freedom to look death straight in the eyes. Art, politics, philosophy struggle with chaos, with crude primordial being. But whence are we to find the strength for this? Heidegger's metaphysics are linked with the finitude of human existence. There is in man no break-through into the infinite; the world is a world of care, of fear, of abandonment, of the dull prosaic—a terrible world. It is the metaphysics of God-forsakenness at its extreme limit. But the divine does not appear under any sort of pseudonym as in Feuerbach, Stirner, Nietzsche and Marx, and there is no satisfaction at all to be derived from the world. Heidegger's pessimism is more consistent and more terrible than the pessimism of Schopenhauer, who was aware of some consolation.

The triune being of God is not only a dogmatic formula, it is a truth of theological scholasticism, and it has a profound existential meaning. Three is a sacred number because it indicates completeness, the surmounting of all duality and division. The whole distinctive character of Christianity lies in the fact that it is not pure monism; it was precisely this which aroused the opposition and hostility of conservative Judaism. The purely monistic tendency in Christianity is Islam or else a return to Judaism. The triune nature of God points to an interior spiritual life in Him and this life is in the whole world. The revelation of the Triune God is the antithesis of the conception of God as pure act, as abstract being which does not display within itself any concrete existence. There is in the Holy Trinity the One and there is his Other, and there is an egress, an issue, a solution in the Third.

It is said of Hegel that he replaced the Christian religious Trinity by a purely philosophical trinity in which the religious meaning is lost. But it would be truer to say that Hegel's trinity was taken from Christian religious experience and given a philosophical expression. The philosophy depends upon religion. The eternal Humanity is the divine Other, the Second Person of the Godhead. Human and cosmic community in freedom and love is the solution of the divine Trinity, the Third Person of the Godhead.

That which, exoterically, is called the creation of the world is the interior life of God, and this must not be reduced to identification, to monism, to pantheism. Here we are faced with an antinomy which is rationally insoluble. Pantheism is rationalization. There are two natures, the divine and the human, which are not to be identified. But both these natures are in the divine Trinity. The divine Other is eternal. Divine humanity and divine Trinity are mysteriously united, the mystery of two (God-man) and the mystery of three (the divine Trinity). The mystery of the divine Trinity is the antithesis of the conception of God as master and a wielder of power, as an autocratic monarch. In God there is not only unity but also ideal plurality. In all the heretical deviations of the first centuries which quarrelled about the intellectual expression of divine mysteries there was partial truth. Especially in Sabellianism, condemned as it was by the mind of the Church, there was truth, though not the complete truth. The Trinity is a *modus* of revelation of the one God and of the epoch of revelation. But for rational thought which is accustomed to think in concepts, here everything is on a razor edge and what is true easily passes into error, and the erroneous may disclose what is true. The distinction which Eckhardt and German mysticism make between *Gottheit* and *Gott*, and which derives from apophatic theology, has been of immense importance. There is a divine Mystery which is inexpressible, and lies beyond the Creator and creation, and there is the Mystery of the Trinity which is directed towards the world. The God Who reveals Himself to the world and to man is not the Absolute; the Absolute cannot have relation within anything at all; the Absolute is an inexpressible Mystery. The Godhead (*Gottheit*) is an inexpressible Mystery in which, we believe, everything will be resolved. But God (*Gott*) is a Mystery which tends to reveal itself.

We are not speaking of various Gods but of one and the same God Who hides Himself and reveals Himself in different degrees. And the distinction here lies not in the object but in the subject. In the history of the religious thought of man and human societies an objectivation of God takes place. Kataphatic theology is concerned with a God who has been objectivized. To this corresponds a certain stage in the socialization of Christianity. But apophatic or mystical theology surmounts the limits of the objectivized conception of God, and liberates it from distorting anthropomorphism, from the interpretation of the relations between God and man in terms of state and authority, of legal procedure and punishment. Feuerbach's idea that man ascribes to God his own highest nature, is not an argument in favour of the denial of God; on the contrary, it is more the other way. It does no more than point out that there does exist a commensurability between God and man, not man however as a natural and social creature, but man as free spirit. The existential dialectic of the divine Trinity, as also the dialectic of the divine and the human, takes place in the very depths of existence.

The dialectic of the Divine Trinity presupposes epochs of trinitarian revelation, that is to say it leads to the admission of the possibility, and even of the necessity of a third revelation. But this means that the two preceding epochs are to be interpreted in the light of the Trinity, that is to say in the light of the revelation of the Spirit as the final revelation. It is only in the Spirit that the revelation of the Deity and of God-manhood is completed and crowned; and this is a revelation of freedom, of love, of creativeness, a revelation of that which God created. Thus there comes about the combination of apophatic mystical theology with existential kataphatic anthropology. The controversies about the transcendent and the immanent which led by way of German idealism to a number of movements in Catholic and Protestant modernism are entirely out of date.[1] The doctrine of immanence in Hegel or E. Hartmann, of a clear-cut monistic type, lies outside the problem which interests me now, the problem of God-manhood.

The old doctrine of immanence, like the old evolutionism, did not understand the catastrophic interrupting moment in spiritual experience and the break on the spiritual path. In this respect the appearance of Kierkegaard was of great importance. Existential philosophy, if it goes deep down into the existence of the subject and is based upon spiritual experience, cannot be an immanent philosophy in the nineteenth century sense. But here we encounter contradictions and antinomies. The revelation of the divine in man and the exaltation of the human to the divine is in character an interruption, an act of transcending. There exists a spiritual experience of the transcendent and of transcending in man. This it is impossible to deny without violence to the reality of experience. Man is a creature who transcends himself, who goes out beyond his own limits, and has eager aspiration to mystery and infinity. But the experience of the transcendent and of transcending is an inward spiritual experience, and in this sense it may be called immanent. And here by immanence is meant not rest within its

[1] On the other hand such existential philosophers as Sartre (but not Heidegger) used the word 'transcendent' completely incorrectly and arbitrarily.

own boundaries but a going-out beyond those boundaries. The transcendent reaches man not from without but from within, out of the depths. God is more deeply within me than I am myself. That was already said by St Augustine. I must transcend to my very self. The deep may be concealed in man, and this deep requires a break-through, a transcending. Through the transcending the mysterious becomes clear, and this is revelation.

The revelation of the transcendent is not an evolutionary process; it is a tragic process in the world. Revelation is objectivized and socialized and then it becomes immanent at the level of human thought and society. Prophet, apostle, saint, mystic pass beyond the frontiers of this evil immanence. People speak of the immanentism of the mystic, but this immanentism has nothing in common with the immanentism of the dully familiar every-day social experience, the immanentism of limited consciousness. The revelation of the transcendent in the world is not evolution, but it presupposes epochs, degrees, both in relation to the individual man and in relation to the history of mankind, and we stand on the borderline between the dying old epoch and the rise of a new epoch of revelation, of a new æon. That which comes to pass in the depths of man comes to pass in the depths of God also. When we think about matters which reach out beyond the limits of thought, outbreaks, which may take various directions, always happen as the outcome of attempts to rationalize the mystery, in which we find support; that is to say from the translation into the language of concepts of that which is inexpressible in concepts. But this does not mean that we can say nothing in human speech. In human speech the Logos is present, although not completely, and movement towards the frontiers, towards the mystery, is possible in thought and speech. The final ideas exist. But the process of thought must be impregnated by integral spiritual experience. Agnosticism is an erroneous limiting of human possibilities. Gnosticism must be affirmed but it must be existential gnosticism. The old gnosticism of the first centuries, in which there was a warping of spiritual experience, dealt with myths. We also have to deal with myths, we must not be limited by concepts. But our myths are of another kind, not the old cosmic myths associated with paganism. No, the fundamental myth is the myth of the divine-human and God-manhood, and this myth is realistic.

A static conception of God cannot be maintained. The Christian God in particular, the God of the religion of crucified Truth can be understood only dynamically. In God there is a creative dynamic process which is accomplished in eternity. This must not be understood as meaning that God depends upon the world and the process that goes on in the world, but that the process which goes on in the world is inwardly linked with the process which goes on in God, in eternity not in time; that is to say it is linked with the divine drama, and it is on this account only that what happens in the world and in man acquires an eternal meaning. A world and man which were on no grounds at all necessary to God would be a mere matter of chance and by that very fact would be destitute of all meaning. We must be bold enough to recognize God's need of man, and such a need by no means limits God. What actually would not only limit God but also degrade Him is a stony, insensitive immobility and self-sufficiency. There is in God a yearning for the loved one and this confers the highest significance upon the loved one. Belief in God is belief in the highest Truth and Right, exalted above the wrongness of the world. But this Truth demands the creative participation of man and of the world. It is divine-human; in it the ideal humanity operates.

In this conjunction of the absolute Truth of God with human truth is hidden the whole mystery of religious life. Various intellectual and optimistic justifications of life have been put forward by men; they have justified life either by the traditional theological idea of divine Providence which is everywhere present (God in everything) or by means of the idealistic pantheistic idea of a world development of spirit, of Reason, which is the idea of Hegel, Schelling and other great idealists, or again by means of the positivist idea of world progress towards a perfect, more rational, free and just life in the future. What in actual fact these forms of justification did was to reflect the irrational principles in this phenomenal world. They have not explained the existence of the evil which triumphs in the world; they have not discerned the tragic character of the world process, and they provided no possibility of constructing a theodicy. To me what seem most incomprehenisble are all forms of historical pantheism, which is more widespread than is commonly understood, and which makes its appearance in even the most orthodox theological teaching. Not pantheism, but dualism is true for our phenomenal world, for within it a struggle of polar opposite principles is going on. But this dualism is not final. The last word, the word as yet unspoken, belongs to God and to divine Truth, it lies beyond human optimism and pessimism; and this is our final faith. This overcomes the tragedy born of freedom which has been the path of man and of the world included in him. To that world beyond, no dualism, no division into paradise and hell, which smacks too much of here and now, can be transferred.

The fall of man gives rise, not to a legal process between God and man, in the sort of way it appears to limited consciousness, but to a dramatic struggle, the creative effort of man responds to the appeal of God. It is not only God Who acts in the world, nor only the freedom of man, but also Fate. This Fate indicates a falling away into the external sphere; it signifies a mysterious God-forsakenness. But this is only the path. For Christian consciousness, for the religion of the Spirit, Fate is a thing which can be overcome. As a matter of logic, it would be inconsistent to say that the process in time enriches eternity, for eternity embraces time. But what is inconsistent in the sphere of logic may have an existential meaning for us.

CHAPTER III

Development and Newness

It is impossible to deny the actual fact of development and recognition of it certainly does not mean the recognition of the theory of evolution as it was expressed in the evolutionary theories of the second half of the nineteenth century. The life of the world is above all, movement, change of position in space and time, and it is an astonishing thing that the fact of development was so tardily observed by human thought. Though it must be said that already in Greek thought there were the germs of a doctrine of development. In the opinion of Heraclitus everything is a stream of change, all things are in a state of flux. But it was the static ontology of Parmenides and Plato which prevailed. Aristotle's doctrine of potency and act may be understood as an attempt at an explanation of the change which takes place in the world. The great idealists of the beginning of the nineteenth century, Schelling, Hegel and others had a doctrine of development, but it was not put in a naturalistic form. In their view it was development of spirit.

The naturalistic doctrine of evolution, on the other hand, had its source in the biological sciences. And this is easily understood since that which develops is, above all, life. Life always has a tendency either to growth and development or to decay and death. Everything which is alive develops. There is no immobility in the world, everything changes and develops, but there exists also a *vis inertiae* which is opposition to all change and hostility to everything new. Life in the world is organized and develops in the direction of higher forms. The irrational elemental is the source of life which can be organized, but at the same time it puts up a resistance to final rationalization. It is not only development the rise of that which did not exist before, which belongs to human life; there is also a process of hardening, of mineralization. Two diametrically opposed principles struggle in life. One's attitude to the change which takes place in the world must be two-fold. Life is change and without the new there is no life. But change may be betrayal. The realization of human personality presupposes change and newness but it also presupposes the unchanging without which there is no personality. In the development of personality man must be true to himself; he must not betray himself; he must preserve his own features which are foreordained for eternity. It is a necessary thing in life that the process of change which leads to the new shall be combined with fidelity.

I have already said that the recognition of the fundamental fact of development in life by no means requires an evolutionary theory in the manner of Darwin, Herbert Spencer and Haeckel. That kind of theory of evolution is out of date both scientifically and philosophically. The evolutionism of the nineteenth century was a form of naturalistic determinism and was never able to explain the origins of evolution. It spoke of the results of evolution, of forms of change, but not of origins and causes. In the evolutionary theory of the nineteenth century no subject of development existed, no inner factor of development. Evolutionism is, in fact, a conservative theory and it denies creativeness in the world. It recognizes merely a redistribution of the parts of the world. Change takes place as the effect of impulses from outside, and no change is ever detected which happens within, from interior activity, from freedom. The external influences, the jolts from outside go on for ever, the inward is never reached, there is no core of any sort which posesses creative energy. But the real development, which the evolutionary theory takes as coming from outside is the result of an inner creative process. Evolution is merely the expression in the horizontal plane, of creative acts which are accomplished in the vertical, in depth.

Dialectic materialism in the form it has taken in Soviet Russia has been an attempt to introduce correctives into the theory of evolution and to recognize self-movement within. Thus matter was endowed with qualities of spirit, with creative activity, with freedom, and intelligence. In this way violence was done to language. A thoroughgoing transvaluation of naturalistic determinism is required. Laws of nature do not exist, laws that is, which dominate the world and man like tyrants. All that exists is a direction in the action of forces which in a given co-relation act uniformly as regards their results. A change in the direction of the forces may change the uniformity. In the primary basis of these forces there lies a spiritual principle, the noumenal. The material world is only the exteriorization and objectivization of spiritual principles. It is a process of induration, of fettering. It might be said that the laws are only the habits of the acting forces, and frequently bad habits. The triumph of new spiritual forces may change the effect of the measured tread of necessity. It may bring about creative newness.

Hegel's doctrine of dialectic development went a great deal deeper than the evolutionary teaching of the second half of the nineteenth century, and it is not naturalistic in character. It is dialectic development of spirit, and it takes place in accordance with a three-fold scheme of thesis, antithesis and synthesis. Development is conditioned by interior opposition which demands solution. The pain of denial plays an enormous part in Hegel's dialectic. The dialectic, the dynamism, are determined by the fact that there is an *other* and this goes very deep. To the smooth-working evolutionary theory there is no *other* and, therefore, no real dynamism. Hegelian monism, which affirms the unity of being and non-being, the identity of opposites, as distinct from the monism of Spinoza, is dynamic. In Hegel's philosophy explosive materials were in preparation, in spite of the fact that Hegel himself was a conservative in politics. His mistake was that he believed in an immanent resolution of the dialectic of opposites, whereas the dialectic of opposites requires the transcendent. Immamentism blunts the edge of the dialectic contradictions. The smooth naturalistic evolutionary theory recognizes no contradictions at all. Dialectic development through contradiction contains a great truth. The path of history lies in it, and in it the destiny of man is worked out.

But with Hegel freedom is not a cause of development, it is a result of development. Freedom is the outcome of necessity, it is recognized necessity. The Hegelian doctrine of dialectic development is, all the same, determinism, not naturalistic determinism, however, but logical. The process of becoming is the logically necessary and inevitable result of the co-relation of being and non-being. Kierkegaard sought to break free from determinism and in his view everything new happens through leaps, but this means that everything new happens as the result of freedom, and through freedom. Evolution in whatever way we understand it is always objectivization and it is this which distinguishes it from creativeness. The title of Bergson's book, *L'Evolution créatrice*, is debatable and is evidence of the naturalistic elements in his metaphysics. Creativeness belongs to the realm of freedom while evolution belongs to the realm of necessity. I have already said that the old evolutionism is obliged to deny the possibility of creative newness. It is shackled in the immanent to the cycle of cosmic forces.

The rise of what is new, of what had not been before, is the greatest mystery in the life of the world. Not only the closed circle of nature, but also the deeper closed circle of being, cannot permit and cannot explain the rise of newness. The mystery of the rise of newness is connected with the mystery of freedom, which is not to be derived from being. The creative act of freedom is a break-through in the natural phenomenal world. It issues from the noumenal world. The creative act of freedom is not a result of development. Development is the result of the creative act of freedom which is objectivized. It is a mystery which begins to reveal itself through movement into the depth, into the fathomless deeps, not through movement into the external, as in the evolutionary theory. The fall of the objectivized world, in which necessity and fate reign, was determined by the direction of freedom in the depth, by the disrupture of God-manhood; and the uplifting impulse is achieved through the re-establishment of the divine-human link. The created world is a world of possibilities; it is not a ready-made finished static world. In it the creative process has to be continued and it has to be continued through man. All the possibilities ought to be disclosed and realized. And, therefore, creative development in the world must be understood as the eighth day of creation. The creation of the world is not only a process which moves from God to man. God demands creative newness from man; He awaits the works of human freedom.

The process of development must be applied also to the history of religion and the history of Christianity. It is impossible to understand Christianity in a static way. As I have already said there exist epochs of revelation, there exist æons of world history. There is creative inspiration in the acceptance of revelation; and its humanizing in terms of the highest humanity, which is God humanity, is also a fact. Development in Christianity has been two-fold. On the one hand it has been improvement, enrichment, creativeness, real newness has made its appearance; and on the other hand it has also been deterioration, distortion, adaptation to the average human level, treachery to its origins, departure from its primitive nature. And one must be able to draw the distinction. Cardinal Newman and Vladimir Solovëv recognized the possibility of the development of dogmas, the fuller disclosure of what had hitherto been insufficiently disclosed. But they did not give this adequate recognition, they did not draw thoroughgoing conclusions from it. The development of Christianity in th world is a complex divine-human process and it must be under stood in the light of divine-humanity. The sources of revelatio ought ever to be understood in a newer and stronger light. Chang of consciousness, the unfolding disclosure of the real huma nature, the growing complexity and refinement of the soul lead t this, that new light is shed upon religious truth; which is to sa that revelation, which issues from eternal Truth, is not give statically in a final completed form, and that it has an inner history

Connected with all this is the question of modernist movement in Christian thought during the nineteenth and twentieth cen turies. The very word 'modernism' has the defect of producing a impression of the subjection of the eternal to the temporal Whereas the very point under discussion is emancipation from th claims of the power of the temporal and historical, and growt towards the eternal. What has given itself out as eternal in reli gious life has too often been the power of the temporal, that is t say, a deficiency of spirituality. For this reason I prefer not t make use of the word 'modernism', but to use the word 'pneu matism'. Modernism is right in this respect, that changes in huma environment and human consciousness take place, and in depend ence upon those changes the reception of revelation also changes The burden of historical stratification is overcome; the way i made possible for new revelations, or more truly, for the on revelation, for the crowning revelation of the Spirit.

Modernist movements have been particularly concerned wit the relation of Christianity to the terrible increase of scientifi knowledge and to changes in social life. These movements hav not reached down into the depths, but they have been of use as purifying and preparatory process. The faith of man has to go forward through criticism, through struggles of the spirit; it i only thus that it acquires the highest value. Man moves forwar through doubt, through dichotomy, through suffering, and only in the overcoming of them all does he become spiritually tempered and ready for the highest degree of spirituality. Dostoyevsky was fond of saying that his faith passed through a refining furnace of doubt, of which the superficially godless were unaware. That which takes place in man and with man in history has an immense importance for the plenitude of divine-human truth. The world changes in accordance with the standpoint from which it is viewed, from what stage of growth, what environment, what class, what religious confession, etc. Nor is it only the view of the world which changes; the view of what is revealed of the other world, the higher world, changes also. Everything changes in dependence upon the height to which men rise or the depth to which they sink, upon the creative development of man or upon the low level of man and his fall. Men have desired to stabilize the truth of revelation in correspondence with the average normal thought of man, which they have identified with eternal human nature, and the truth of revelation has appeared in a static, petrified form. A veto has been imposed upon creativeness. Men have not desired it. They have been afraid to acknowledge the creative nature of man and the possibility of the new. The new that was bad has all the same come to pass, but the possibility of what is new and good has been suppressed. In this way an ossification of Christianity has been brought about, a mortifying and extinguishing of the spirit. But it was said: 'Quench not the Spirit.' That which does not move forward, which does not develop towards the newness of the Kingdom of God, goes backward and is turned into mineral. Truth is the way and the life and not a thing in the world of objects.

The history of the European soul has been dynamic, and great changes have taken place in it. By no means the same soul now faces Christianity which faced the Christianity of the Middle Ages or of the first Christians. An entirely different sensitiveness has been revealed in it. Much that is new in the human soul has been disclosed in Petrarch, in Rousseau, in the Romantics at the beginning of the nineteenth century, in Dostoyevsky, in Kierkegaard, Nietzsche, Ibsen, and the Symbolists at the end of the nineteenth century, and in the generation of Communists at the beginning of the twentieth century. It is impossible not to take account of the experience which has come to light in the most significant intellectual movements of our time. Such are Heidegger and existential philosophy, Freud and psycho-analysis, Karl Barth and dialectic theology, Husserl and phenomenology, racialism and totalitarianism, marxism and communism. Those who have had the most influence, and have wielded power over the soul, were Nietzsche, Marx and Kierkegaard. The old Christian catechisms had no answer to give to the new problems and the new restlessness. In the early centuries of Christianity the doctors of the Church gave answers to the problems which were raised by the heresies of that time. Our era knows no heresies like the ancient heresies, but heresies of a quite different character are arising, of which those who remain within the Christian dogmatic system are not aware, and they demand a Christian answer. Such an answer cannot be provided by necrotic forms of historical Christianity. Such subjects as the creative venturesomeness of man, the entirely new forms of evil, do not lend themselves to solution by the old standardized ethics. The attraction of the abyss of non-being, the unprecedented freedom unknown to former ages, the transition from freedom to slavery, the mystery of personality and its destruction, contemporary society on earth and its temptations; and many other forms of human self-assertion and pride have become different and more frightful than they were in the past.

In a word the psychical element in man has undergone great changes. The anthropology of the old patristic literature does not now correspond to the state of contemporary man, who has undergone a complex development. Energies which had been idden in the deep strata of the soul have been brought out into the pen. But this development is highly complex and has two sides o it. On the one hand man is being deepened; on the other hand e is being thrown up on the surface. The emotional side of man's ature on the one hand, from the time of Rousseau and the Ronantics, has been much strengthened and developed in comparison vith previous centuries. On the other hand it is weakened and ppressed by the power of technical skill, by the chilling touch of netal.

This complexity is particularly evident in relation to moral levelopment. It would be untrue to say that there is such a thing s a process which brings man and human societies to a state of noral perfection along a progressively rising line. Moral regress lso takes place. All the time newer and newer forms of human rutality are being revealed, forms more subtle and repellent. Moral consciousness in the past permitted torture, and this was lue to beliefs which were superstitious. But in the light of presentlay moral consciousness torture shows itself as a much more terible thing. In former ages men were often better. Nevertheless, rogress in moral consciousness does exist. Humaneness is a new henomenon; it is a result of the inner underground activity of Christianity. Man is becoming more abominable morally than in he less humane and harsher past. But it is a new consciousness vhich now passes judgment on him. Modernism can be bad because it can be associated with fashion and imitation, with slavery o time. Aesthetic sensitiveness and refinement may grow, but a hift of direction in art does not mean progress. It is quite imposible to say that present-day writers stand on a higher level of levelopment than Sophocles, Dante or Shakespeare. The successive changes which run through classicism, romanticism, realism, ymbolism, surrealism, expressionism, and the rest, do not represent development, but the history of the human soul and they are reflection of its quest. Evolution does not unfailingly mean progress, movement towards the highest goal, to the Kingdom c God. It may even mean regress. Newness does not without fa mean amelioration and the attainment of higher value. The cu of the new, *qua* new, is just as bad a thing as the cult of the pas *qua* past. Real religious newness can be associated only with a nev era of the Spirit. And that is a new era of revelation, which cannc be the action of God only, but must be also the action of man, h creative act. It is possible to talk about this only if a dynamic con ception both of the life of the world and of the life of God b admitted. The prospect of unending development in the future, a accepted, for instance, in the doctrine of progress advanced b Condorcet and others, is false. But the idea of progress may fin support not in another infinity, but in an end. For that reason deeper conception of development relies upon eschatology.

CHAPTER IV

Fear

We have spoken so far about that which is above. Now something must be said about that which is beneath.[1] Fear lies at the roots of the life of this world. There was the 'terror antiquus'—the ancient fear, which corresponds to the German *Angst* and the French *angoisse*. The actual terminology, which dintinguishes between *Angst* and *Furcht*, is derived in the main from Kierkegaard. Among the many definitions of man one may be included which defines him as a creature who is put to the test of fear. And this might be said of every living thing. The fear felt by animals is horrible. It is a grievous thing to look into the eyes of a frightened animal. Fear is due to the dangerous and threatening condition of life in the world. And the nearer to perfection the life is, the more individualized it is, so much the more it is liable to threat, and exposed to great dangers, so much the more is death its lot. The necessity of defending oneself against danger is always present. The organism is to a remarkable degree constructed for defence. The struggle for existence, of which life is full, presupposes fear.

It is a mistake to think that courage and fear entirely exclude each other. Courage is not so much the absence of fear, as victory over fear, and what is more, over fear acting in a particular direction. A man may be very brave in one set of circumstances and a coward in another; for example, very brave in war, and a coward when facing his own wife. He may be a hero and show no fear of death, and yet experience fear when face to face with a

[1] See Keyserling, *Méditations sud-américaines*; Kierkegaard, *Le concept d'angoisse*; Heidegger, *Sein und Zeit*.

mouse, or a caterpillar, or an infectious disease. He may be extraordinarily brave in a battle of ideas, and be afraid when faced by material difficulties. There are people who are very brave in a physical sense and very cowardly in a moral sense, and *vice versa*. A man may attain a high degree of bravery in one particular sphere of life, and abandon other spheres in a state of fear.

But everywhere and in everything, victory over fear remains a spiritual problem, the problem of conquering a thing which debases man. An incalculable amount of violence and cruelty in human life is the outcome of fear. 'Terror' is not only a cause of fear in those against whom it is directed, but it also indicates fear in those who practise it. It is well known that people who are possessed by a persecution mania not only experience fear, but also start persecuting others and throw them into a state of fear. The most terrible of people are those who are possessed by fear. Fear operates destructively. Fear is indissolubly linked with time, with what the future will be, with what is a menace arising from change in time. In the future there may be suffering, and there certainly will be death, which is the most terrible of the things which threaten life. A great number of ancient pagan beliefs and superstitions were connected with fear and strong desire.

In Kierkegaard's view, and in Heidegger's who in this respect follows him, *Angst* places us face to face with the abyss of non-being.[1] It is an event on the boundary, on the frontier line between the external primitive world and the supra-ego. To these philosophers *angoisse* is our reaction when faced by somebody or something which seems to us to threaten to destroy our own *Dasein*. *Angst*, on the other hand, is not evoked by anything definite; it places us face to face with the world pure and simple. According to Heidegger *Dasein* takes refuge in *Das Man*, from the unknown and the strange. Fear is an oppression which has fallen upon the world's heart. In his view *Dasein* is anxiety, i.e. being

[1] See the excellent book, Woehlens, *La Philosophie de Martin Heidegger*.

which is thrown out into the world, in which it is lost. Anxiety is continual death. The acceptance of death is something akin to Nietzsche's *amor fati*. Moral consciousness rises above *Das Man* and destroys him. Where does this idea of Heidegger's come from? *Angst* is connected with nothingness. *Das Nichts selbst nichtet.* In Kierkegaard *Angst* has more of a psychological character, whilst in Heidegger it is cosmic. But horror in the face of death and nothingness can only exist when personality exists, such horror exists for personality only.

In Heidegger everything comes from below, not from above; indeed for him there is no above in any sense. It is left unexplained where the higher and discriminating element comes from, but all the same it is there in his thought. This is a point which Nietzsche also does not explain. In this respect Kierkegaard's position is better. Fear is the outcome of being Godforsaken. But whether it is a matter of the world and man being abandoned by God, or of God being abandoned by the world and man, in any case a state of being Godforsaken presupposes the existence of God. Faced by the abyss of nothingness, man experiences fear and horror because he is separated from God. Fear is the result of sundering, separating, alienation, abandonment. Psychologically, fear is always the fear of suffering. Man experiences fear and horror when through suffering he comes upon an insurmountable wall beyond which is non-being, emptiness, nothingness. This has nothing in common with the Nirvana of Buddhism, which is egress and enlightenment.[1] Neither is this horror-fear to be confused with what Otto calls *Mysterium tremendum*, and which means a primary sense of the Divine.[2]

The paradoxical nature of the position lies in the fact that it is precisely that which liberates from suffering, namely non-being, emptiness, nothingness, which also evokes the greatest horror.

[1] See Suzini, *Essais sur le Bouddhisme, Zen.*
[2] See R. Otto, *Das Heilige.*

A distinction must be drawn between animal fear, which is associated with a lower condition of life, and spiritual fear which belongs to the higher conditions. There is a fear which is born of the menace of the lower world. And there is a fear which arises from the force exerted by the higher world, the fear of God, for which another word is needed. God is a consuming fire.

Epicurus thought that he was overthrowing religion when he said that it had its origin in fear. But fear is a much more serious and profound condition of the spirit than he supposed. He had not read Kierkegaard and many others. The first stages of the revelation of the Divine in the world are associated with fear. They were conditioned by the low state of man, by his submersion in the lower world, by the feebleness of his capacity for thought, by darkness, which stood in fear of the light. The primitive *Mysterium tremendum* was mingled with fear. The fear of God was confused with fear of the world. The religious life of man was filled to the full with fear, although it might be said that the goal of religious life is victory over fear. At the first beginning of things God had to arouse fear although He is also that beneficent power which should free man from that deadly fright which arises from life in the world. Emancipation from fear, from fear of the devil and fear of hell, the liberation and cleansing of the idea of God from the distorting effect of fear, has taken place but slowly even in the thought which is most Christian. The great spiritual task with which man is faced is to achieve emancipation from fear, from superstition, from the tormenting of the devil and of demons, from servile fear of power and might, from the fear of a merciless judgment, from fanaticism and intolerance, from hatred of the foe and from revenge, from the objectivization of evil in oneself. Fear is always fear of the base and the evil, and only in a darkened mind can it appear to be fear of the higher.

Fear governs the world. Power by its very nature avails itself of fear. Human society was built up on fear and, therefore, it was built up on lies, for fear is the father of falsehood. There is such a thing as alarm lest truth should lessen fear and prevent the government of man. Pure truth might lead to the fall of kingdoms and civilizations. Therefore, even Christianity has adjusted itself to fear. Periodically government by fear leads to a totalitarian régime and to Terror. The element of fear enters into all forms of authority, and freedom is the antithesis of fear. The truth about freedom is hidden through fear. The accommodation of truth to the prosaic dullness of everyday experience has taken place from fear. Fear always conceals truth and truth tends to reveal itself when the experience of fear lived through, leads to the overcoming of it, to emancipation. Fear is connected not only with falsehood but also with cruelty. It is not only those who inspire fear who become cruel, but also those who feel it. The masses are not only governed through fear but the masses themselves govern by fear. Fear in the life of society is the mistrust of man; and fear is always conservative although outwardly it has at times been revolutionary in form. The fear of hell in religious life, the fear of revolution, or the loss of property, in social life, lowers the value of everything. Man lives in fear of life and in fear of death. Fear reigns alike in the life of the individual and in the life of society. Anxiety, insecurity of life, in the last resort give rise to fear. But what is most serious is this; fear distorts thought and hinders the knowledge of truth. Man stands face to face with a conflict between fear and truth. Tormented man fears the truth; he thinks that truth will injure him. Fearlessness in the face of truth is the greatest achievement of the spirit. Heroism indeed is fearlessness in the face of truth, in the face of truth and death.

Religious life has been distorted by fear, which has been made use of to uphold various forms of evil, and the unjust ordering of society. When the ancient world was coming to an end it was tormented by the fear of demons and the spirits of nature; and it sought salvation in the mysteries. One of the greatest achievements of Christianity, one which even those who are not Christians are bound to acknowledge, has been to set man free from demonolatry and the fears with which it had enslaved him. Magic did not help, it simply meant dependence upon cosmic forces. But the ancient fear made its way even into Christianity and the old demons and their chief, the devil, began to torment Christians too. The fear of the lower was intermingled with fear of the higher, and fear of the devil with the fear of God. The distinction between *Furcht* (*peur*) and *Angst* (*angoisse*) slipped into the background; the emotions aroused by the lower cosmic and social forces were transferred to God, and this is what I call cosmomorphism and sociomorphism. The ancient fear was crystallized into doctrine, and so it is not so easy to free Christian doctrine from fear. Fear was placed on a higher level than the virtue of kindliness, which was looked upon with dread as though it were a weakness.

Christian theology has been accused of intellectualism, and justly so; the intellect can never be divorced from feeling and will. Official theological doctrines have been distorted by the emotion of fear, and this emotion determines them to a much greater degree than the intellect. Present-day psychopathology is doing a great deal for the study of fears, and of every kind of phobia, and in this way it can render the service of purifying religious thought and liberating it from the fears which harrow it. Within the confines of this phenomenal world it is probably impossible to be finally set free from fear, for the position of man remains menacing. But it is possible to be freed from the transference of those fears to religious life and to one's relation to God. It is possible to be liberated from a confusion of the lower fear with the higher condition of shrinking awe and anguish. Kierkegaard defines *Angst* as the dizziness of freedom. With him nothingness, non-being, acquires a positive meaning also, and does not remain simply negative. This could not be said of fear. But Hegel understood better than anybody that without non-being there is no becoming.

Fear always has a relation to suffering; it is experienced as suffering, and it is the dread of suffering. Of suffering I shall speak in the following chapter. But it is impossible to dissociate fear from this central fact of human life. Man is dragged away from the higher world and subjected to the lower world. This inevitably gives rise to fear and suffering. But the connection with the lower world is so close that the higher world itself begins to present itself in the fashion of the lower world. Fear and suffering, the products of the lower world which enslaves man, may be experienced as though they were derived from the higher world, which ought to be a liberating power. Jacob Boehme very well said that the love of God operates in the darkness, as a burning fire. Fear lowers the dignity of man, the dignity of free spirit. Fear has always been regarded as shameful in war; it is then called cowardice. Man has reached the stage of overcoming fear in war; he has performed miracles of bravery; he has become a hero. But great difficulty has been found in extending this to all the rest of life and especially to the life of the spirit. One cannot repeat often enough that emancipation from fear is the chief spiritual task of man. The attainment of fearlessness is the highest condition of man, and it is a question of attainment, for no one can say that fear is entirely unknown to him.

The fact of fear is connected with the inter-relation among the conscious, the sub-conscious, and the supra-conscious. Fear issues from the depth of the sub-conscious, from the ancient origins of man. Consciousness may enhance fear, a quickened consciousness is associated with fear. It is only from the supra-conscious that the final and decisive victory over fear comes. It is a triumph of the spirit. It has been said that 'perfect love casteth out fear', but perfect love is so rare that fear continues to govern human life. The fear in eros love is very powerful; it exists in the depth of the sex life. Fear distorts the human, and in this lies the complexity of the God-human process.

CHAPTER V

Suffering

I suffer, therefore, I exist. This is truer and more profound than the *cogito* of Descartes. Suffering is linked with the very existence of personality and personal consciousness. Boehme says that suffering, *Qual*, *Quelle*, *Qualität*, is the source of the creation of things.[1] Suffering is associated not only with the helpless animal condition of man, that is to say with his lower nature, but also with his spirituality, with his freedom, his personality, that is with his higher nature. The refusal of spirituality and of freedom, the refusal of personality might mitigate suffering and lessen pain, but it would mean a refusal of the dignity of man. And indeed the precipitation of man into the lower animal state saves him from nothing whatever, because life in this world does not take care of itself nor protect itself. The wastage of life in the world is appalling, the meaningless perishing of innumerable lives which are doomed to carry on a torturing struggle for existence. No salvation from suffering is to be found by plunging into the biological sphere of existence. Suffering is the basic fact of human existence. In this world the fate of all life which has attained to individuality is suffering. Man is born with pain, with pain he dies, suffering accompanies the two most notable events in human life. Sickness, perhaps the greatest of evils, continually lies in wait for man.

It is not without good grounds that psycho-analysts speak of the traumatism of the process of birth, of the fright and the anguish which man experiences as soon as he arrives in this world.[2]

[1] Hegel speaks of this in his great *Logic*.
[2] See Otto Ronx, *Le Traumatisme de la naissance*.

Buddha taught that all desire begets suffering; but life is desire; the acceptance of life is the acceptance of suffering. One's disquietude about the suffering which goes hand in hand with life, and one's sympathy, ought not to be limited to the human world alone. The fear of animals is horrible and they are more helpless than human beings. There is nothing more absurd than the Cartesian teaching that animals are mere automata. The duty of man in relation to the animal world has not been adequately brought to light in Christianity. In that respect Buddhism has been on a higher level. Man has his obligation to cosmic life; the guilt lies at his door. When my dear Muri, my favourite cat, died, and cried out in its death agony, I felt the suffering of the world, the suffering of every living thing, and I was a sharer in that suffering. Everyone shares or ought to share the suffering of others and that of the whole world.

Suffering is a fundamental theme in all religions of redemption, and indeed it is a basic religious theme in general. In suffering man passes through moments of Godforsakenness. On the other hand through suffering he arrives at communion with God. Suffering may pass over into joy. Man is terribly unhappy on this earth, terribly frightened; he experiences horror and agony; and every living thing is in the same position. But man possesses the power to create, to rise to heroic achievements, to experience ecstasy. He is a degraded creature and also an exalted creature. Pascal understood this better than anyone. The impossibility of enthusiasm and of ecstasy is a source of suffering, it is a state of division, an enfeeblement of the creative life. Unhappiness is above all a state of disruption and division. The fundamental and most serious question of human existence is, how is one to triumph over suffering, how is suffering to be endured, how is one to avoid being crushed by it, how is the amount of suffering for all men and for the whole of life to be decreased? There were already religions of a suffering god before Christianity, such as the religions of Osiris, Dionysus and others. There is a suffering of the god himself and it is a saving suffering. The mystery of Christianity arises from this. But theological doctrines have always been afraid to recognize suffering in God, and have condemned what is known as patripassianism. But here too, as in every case which brings us into contact with mystery, everything is on a razor-edge, for the suffering of the Son of God, of the God-man, is acknowledged. Here everything turns upon the union of the suffering of the human with the suffering of the divine, for in that the disruption and alienation between the human and the divine is overcome.

Why is it that man suffers so much in this world? And is it possible to justify God in view of such an amount of suffering? That is the question which Dostoyevsky set so painfully before himself. Radishchev, the father of the Russian intelligentsia, was from his early years profoundly shaken by human suffering. It is a very Russian theme. Pity for those who suffer, sympathy with those who suffer undeservedly, is experienced to begin with as Godforsakenness, and later leads to the struggle against God. The fundamental question here is the theme of unmerited suffering. It is set out in the Book of Job, and God forbid that we should be like Job's comforters. There is suffering in the world which is not a punishment for sin. The most obvious suffering is that connected with the body, that body which sets bounds to the infinite aspirations of man, which is sick, grows old, and dies, and with which the painful struggle for existence is associated. Man carries the curse of the body, which promises transient illusory pleasures and is the cause of much suffering. Man is born because sex exists, but for the same reason, he also dies. There are moments of joy, but the fundamental background of life is anxiety and suffering. The Greeks, who are accounted to have been enjoyers of life say through their greatest creative achievement, in the voice of Greek tragedy, that it were better for man not to be born. Goethe and

Tolstoy were most fortunate and externally happy men of genius, but one says that throughout his whole life there had in all been but a few happy hours, while the other wanted to put an end to himself.

By what is suffering to be explained? The contemporary Indian philosopher, Aurobindo, says that suffering is the rejoinder made by the All, the Whole, to the vain attempt of the ego to bring the universal within the possible limits of purely individual joy. Max Scheler says that suffering is the experience of sacrificing the part for the sake of the whole, the sacrifice of the lower value for the sake of the higher; he connects suffering with sacrifice. The possibility of suffering is also connected with a discord between the independent parts and their functional position in the whole.[1] These solutions cannot satisfy human personality set face to face with its own individual fate. They are based upon the complete overwhelming of the individually-personal by the universally-common. Kierkegaard's thought goes a great deal deeper when he says that the suffering of man is connected with the fact that he is lonely. Human beings are divided, as it were, into two classes. There are those who are painfully conscious of the sufferings of the world and of men, and there are those who are comparatively indifferent to them. In the history of European man through the centuries, sensitiveness to suffering and the feeling that it is intolerable have greatly increased. This is true, at least, in respect of a certain more refined section of mankind. It was only after a long delay that man became conscious of the fact that torture and execution and the cruel treatment of criminals was a thing that cannot be permitted. And at the same time we are living in a period which is very cruel, in an epoch of unprecedented suffering.

One must see the source of suffering in the lack of correspondence between the nature of man, and the object world of his environment into which we are thrown; one must see it in the

[1] See Max Scheler, *Le sens de la souffrance.*

unceasing clash of the ego with the non-ego which is alien and indifferent to it, with the opposition of objectivity; that is to say it is to be seen in the objectivization of human existence. If one may speak of a distinction between harmonic and disharmonic human types and states, the fact that man by his position in the world finds himself in a state of disharmony goes still deeper. The painful self-contradiction in man which is the cause of suffering consists in this, that he is in his unrevealed depths a being who is infinite and who is straining towards infinity; a being who is in quest of eternity and is fore-ordained to it; and at the same time by the very conditions of his existence, a being who is finite and limited, temporal and mortal. Man comes crashing against a wall which there is no breaking through. In the depth of human suffering is the experience of insurmountability, inevitability and irrevocability.

The dualism in which man lives in this world is also a source of incalculable suffering. The experience of suffering is the antithesis of the experience of integrality. The violation of the integrality and harmony of the world also gives rise to suffering. But this happens because man meets with a world of objects and only rarely breaks through to the world of subsistences. Within me myself there is much which is alien to me, which is not mine (the 'Es' of Freud) and this element in my very self which is alien to me is a source of suffering. The struggle for the realization of personality is a struggle against the alien in me, which makes a slave of me. There ought to be present in me the whole of God's world and instead of it there is the non-ego, the objectivity which deadens. The source of suffering in man is two-fold; it lies in an insurmountable wall outside him and in an insurmountable wall within him; in the degrading slavery imposed by the alien nature of the world, and in the still more degrading slavery imposed by himself, by that which is non-ego, but appears to man to belong to his ego. It may be accepted as beyond doubt that a large amount of suffering and unhappiness is due to being engulfed by one's ego, to egoism. At the extreme limit this leads to madness which is always a state of being engulfed by one's ego, of being incapable of getting out of it. The capacity to issue from the ego, to escape engulfment by it, is a condition of the realization of personality. The ego is not yet personality. Pascal says that '*le moi est haïssable*'. This could not be said about personality.

The physical and psychical organism of man is only partially adapted to the surrounding environment, which is always a threat to him. Indeed it is a matter of wonder that man acquires the possibility of stable existence in the phenomenal world, in which he finds but few points of support and meets with only a few who are his neighbours. When he experiences the whole cosmos as neighbour to him, as divine, then he finds not this world of objects, this world which is alien to him, but already the other world, which lies beyond this. And the dissociation of man from the primary source of life, from other human beings, from cosmic life, gives rise to suffering. Whereas communion, the finding of community and neighbourliness, are the reverse of suffering. Death is the greatest suffering, probably because it is the passing through a moment of, as it were, absolute dissociation, rupture and isolation. A state of harmony, that is to say the discovery of propinquity and communion, are the antithesis of suffering. The greatest sacrament is the sacrament of Communion, and it is not only a human but also a cosmic sacrament. The fate of man from birth to death remains incomprehensible to us, and the sufferings which fall to his lot are incomprehensible. But this is only a very small fragment of man's destiny in eternity, of his journey through many worlds. If we take a single day of a human life, detached from the days which precede and from those which follow it, we shall understand but little of what happens to the man. But the whole life of a man from birth to death is only a short day in his destiny from the point of view of eternity.

Hegel had some remarkable ideas on the subject of the 'unhappy consciousness'.[1] The unhappy consciousness is separation, dividedness. It has to be passed through in order that the higher consciousness may be reached. But is not all consciousness unhappy? Consciousness always presupposes division, a falling apart into subject and object and a painful dependence upon the object. Dostoyevsky considered suffering as the sole cause of the rise of consciousness. Dostoyevsky, Kierkegaard and Nietzsche are of the greatest interest in this connection. Nietzsche's fight against suffering, against terrible sickness and loneliness, his resistance to them, is the most remarkable thing in his life, and it imparts a heroic character to it. The ethics of antiquity and especially the classical ethics of Aristotle saw in man a being who searches for happiness, blessedness, harmony, and is capable of finding it. This view remains also in Thomas Aquinas and in official Catholic theology. But in actual fact Christianity has made breaches in this conception. In respect of this the evidence of Kant, Schopenhauer, Dostoyevsky, Kierkegaard, and Nietzsche is important. It is not by chance that man, in order to mitigate pain and extinguish suffering, seeks to forget himself and to refuse consciousness, to blunt the edge of it. He tries to do this at times by sinking into the sub-conscious, for example by the use of narcotics, or through the ecstasy which comes from submersion in the elemental animal; at other times by rising to the superconscious, to spiritual ecstasy, to fusion with the divine. There is a limit to the possibility of bearing suffering. Beyond that limit man loses consciousness and in that way, as it were, saves himself.

It is by no means the worst people who suffer most; those who suffer most are the best people. The capacity to suffer may be a sign of greater depth. Development of thought and refinement of soul go hand in hand with intensification of suffering, with greater sensitiveness to pain, not only spiritual but physical pain.

[1] See Jean Wahl, *Le malheur de la conscience dans la philosophie de Hegel.*

also. Unhappiness, suffering, evil, are not direct causes of the awakening of strength in man, and of spiritual growth, but they may contribute to the arousing of his interior strength. Without pain and suffering in this world man would droop and the animal in him would be victorious. This obliges us to think that suffering in this world is not merely evil, the result of evil and the expression of evil. It is entirely wrong to suppose that suffering falls to the lot of man in proportion to his guilt and sin, although this is the theme of many sermons. When we think in that way we are like Job's comforters, but God justified Job, not the comforters. The Book of Job is the great witness to the existence of unmerited suffering, and of the innocent sufferer. Greek tragedy also bears witness to the same thing. Oedipus was not guilty, he was the victim of fate. But more important than all is the guiltless suffering of the Son of God, of the righteous man, Jesus. Divine suffering exists and this divine suffering is evoked by a lack of congruity between God and the condition of the world and man. There is a dark suffering which leads to ruin, and there is a bright suffering which leads to salvation. Christianity changes the path of suffering into the path of salvation. It is divine-human suffering, and that answers the tormenting question of theodicy. Human life is filled with the existential dialectic of suffering and joy, of unhappiness and happiness.

In all this human questioning about suffering, the greatest interest attaches to Buddhism, Stoicism and Christianity, and the three answers which these give are fundamental even to-day. The Stoic conflict with suffering is to be found in the experience of some who know nothing at all about the Stoics. Buddhism and Stoicism do not accept suffering; they seek to get away from it, and by so doing to secure relief from it. Christianity accepts suffering; it accepts the Cross and in the enlightened bearing of suffering it seeks liberation and salvation. Buddhism does not accept the world. It would conquer desire which ties one to the world and seeks to attain Nirvana, which is not non-being, as Western people commonly suppose, but lies beyond being and non-being; it is neither existence nor non-existence. Japanese Buddhism, Zen, expounds the teaching of Buddha not as the repudiation of the will but as illumination, that is to say, as, above all, victory over egocentricity.[1] It might be called modernism. Buddhism has certain great advantages over Brahmanism—it involves sympathy, for instance, a sense of the evil of the world; there is further an absence of ritualism in it, and of the intolerable pride of the Brahman hierarchy. But Buddhism moves away from the life of men and of the world; it does not want man to take its burden upon himself and to bear the cross. Stoicism accepts the world and seeks to reconcile the life of man with the law of the cosmic mind. But it seeks to attain inward liberation from suffering through a change of attitude towards everything which arises from the life of the world and is capable of bringing suffering upon man; it seeks to attain to 'apathy'. Neither Buddhism nor Stoicism seeks to change the world, or to transform it. They take it as it is, and deal with its suffering by changing their attitude to the world, whether by repudiating it or by the attainment of a state of indifference to it. Stoic moral philosophy was a noble thing, but the 'apathy' of Stoicism is non-creative and decadent in character.

Both Buddhist and Stoic elements may be met with even in our entirely different Christian moral philosophy and our Christian attitude to suffering. Christ teaches us to bear the cross of life. Does this mean that we must increase suffering and go in search of it? Of course such is not the meaning of bearing the cross. Bearing the cross which falls to our lot means an enlightened experience of suffering, and that means a lessening of suffering in comparison with the unenlightened, sombre and gloomy experience of it.

[1] On Buddhism, in addition to the classical book by Oldenberg, see De la Vallée-Poussin, *Nirvana*, and the Japanese, Zuziki, *Essais sur le Bouddhisme Zen*.

Elements of sadism and masochism play no small part in religious life and that is one reason why the history of Christianity is so complex. Christ turned suffering into the way of salvation. That which is true and right is crucified in the world. The one sinless righteous Man was crucified. But this does not mean that suffering must be sought, that we must torture ourselves; nor does it mean that it is necessary to inflict suffering upon other people in the interests of their salvation. But all the same there have been profoundly convinced Christians who have at times been very cruel precisely as a result of their faith and on behalf of it. The Inquisition, the use of torture, the justification of the death penalty, and the infliction of cruel punishments, have been based upon this belief in the saving nature of suffering. St Dominic was a cruel Inquisitor, St Theresa behaved cruelly to the insane, Joseph Volotskoy was very cruel and demanded the torture and execution. of heretics. Theophan Zatvornik propagated a policy of cruelty Christians have sought after suffering, sickness, self-torture and the torture of others. This was due to a distorted sense of sin and to fear. In the inquisitors individual personal kindliness might be combined with sadism. The primary source of the terrible gloomy error lay in the assumption that the suffering of man is pleasing and acceptable to God, that is to say in the transference of sadistic feelings to God. Christian souls of earlier days felt suffering less keenly than those of the present day. They were more acutely conscious of the sense of sin; therefore they were less sensitive to suffering. But human life is dependent not only upon necessity; it depends still more upon chance which cannot be explained, upon what is called the ill-starred coincidence of circumstances. The problem by which man is confronted by no means lies in finding an explanation of the suffering of his life, of its meaningless chances, and its crushing necessity, in the fact of his sins, and in seeing all this as a punishment of them. It is the spiritual problem of bearing suffering worthily and of turning the dark and gloomy suffering which leads to perdition into an enlightened sufferin which leads to salvation.

Man is an unconsciously sly and furtive creature and he badly understood, indeed he has but a poor understanding (himself. Man may intensify his suffering in order that he ma suffer less; it is a psychological paradox. It is the existential dialec tic of suffering:—while suffering from one cause a man consol himself by suffering from another. He is capable of performin heroic feats in order that he may suffer less. He goes to war an performs miracles of bravery; he becomes a monk and achieve great feats of ascetism, in order to find distraction from the suffer ing which has been the outcome of an unhappy love affair, o caused by the death of someone near and dear to him. Or h begins to torment the place where he has a pain; he starts intensi fying the pain in order to alleviate pain. He not only flees fron what causes him pain, but he is also attracted to pain and concen trates upon it. Masochism is very much inherent in man; an masochism, like sadism, is a perversion which is begotten b suffering. And this has a mysterious connection with sex, which i a thing which wounds man.

Man is a sick creature, and to this is due the fact that the greates psychological discoveries have been made by psychopathology At one time he is easily disposed to persecution mania, at anothe he has a mania for greatness; the two manias are linked with eacl other in such a way that a man who is possessed by a persecutio mania readily begins to persecute other people. The human con flict with suffering is time and again pathological in character Madness can sometimes be a way of escape from the unresolve conflicts of life, and may provide relief. The most horrible thin in human life is the autonomy and isolation of the various sphere of life of the soul, the breakaway from the centre which subordin ates to a higher meaning, and the formation of isolated worlds Thus the autonomy and isolation of the sexual life leads to th monstrous world depicted by the Marquis de Sade.[1] In the opinion of de Sade man is essentially evil, cruel, and sensual. He thinks that vice and virtue are indifferent from the point of view of Providence. But the formation of other autonomous and isolated spiritual worlds is just as horrible, for example, the world of ambition and love of power, or the world of gain and enrichment, or the world of hatred. The man who in the grip of passion has formed his own autonomous world suffers himself and causes suffering to others. An isolated unspiritualized passion evokes an endless intolerable craving; it is the outcome of a break with the spiritual centre of man and a rupture between the very centre itself and the primary source of life in the world, that is to say in the last resort it always leads to the break-up of God-manhood.

The fear of death is fear of the most intense suffering. To die is to pass through the severance of soul and body, severance from the world and man, and severance from God. The suffering which arises from parting and separation is suffering of a very intense kind. But still greater is the suffering which arises from remorse of conscience and the poignant sense of guilt, the suffering which is born of the irrevocable and irreparable. This is, as it were, an anticipation of the pains of hell. Man seeks for restoration and preservation in the memory of past experience, and many memories are sweet to him. But to a still greater degree he seeks to forget, to let go the memory of what is evil and degrading, and if memory retained the whole past unbroken, man would not be able to bear it. In the same way he would be unable to bear the knowedge and prevision of the future, of sufferings to come, and of the hour of death. Man and the world inevitably pass through crucifixion and death, and this must be accepted in an illumined way. Death exists not only because man is a mortal creature in this world, but also because he is an immortal being who cannot,

[1] See Marquis de Sade, *Les infortunes de la vertu*. One must not deny the talent of de Sade.

within the conditions of this world, bring to actual realization the fullness and eternity of life.

It is merely an exoteric idea that suffering is a punishment for sin. Devilish perversions of Christianity have been the result of the persuasion that suffering is a consequence which sin has earned, that it is a punishment from God. From that it was possible to draw the conclusion that one must cause the greatest possible suffering. In France and England in the Middle Ages the condemned were refused any opportunity of sacramental confession in order that the assurance of eternal hell might be added to the pains of death. The sublimity of Christian Services for the dead and Christian funeral rites provides a striking contrast to this perversion of Christianity with its callousness and lack of pity.

Suffering is of two kinds. There are sufferings which are removed and overcome by changes in the social order and the development of scientific knowledge; it is a necessary thing to carry on the fight against the social causes of suffering and against those sufferings which are due to the boorish ignorance of man. The abolition of social slavery (to which the slavery which exists within the capitalistic system belongs); the guarantee of the right to work and of a worthy existence; the spread of education and technical and medical knowledge; victory over the elemental forces of nature; all these can lessen the amount of suffering. But you cannot organize the supply of happiness, any more than you can organize truth. Happiness is bestowed only as a gracious moment. The gift of truth comes only as the result of a quest and of aspiration to the infinite; it is given as a way and a life; and it is always debatable. It is only the lower, not the higher, that can be organized. Moments of the experience of happiness have something mysterious about them, they are like reminiscences of paradise or a presentiment of it.

But there is a sort of suffering which is connected with the tragic basis of life and has a deep-seated origin. It is not the outcome of a bad social order and cannot be removed by the amelioration of it. It is the suffering which is our tragic lot in the world; it is our fate, and this fate we can overcome only by overcoming this world. A number of Marxian-Communists are arriving at a new humanism and claiming a final victory over fate without having recourse to myths (Christianity in their opinion vanquishes fate through myths). They would vanquish the source of suffering and organize the universal happiness of mankind. It is a mistake to think that Marxism is a social utopia. There is a great deal which Marxism desires which is capable of realization socially, and it ought to be so realized. But Marxism is a spiritual utopia for it is based upon a failure to understand the spiritual conditions of human existence. It is impossible by social means to overcome that fundamental tragic conflict which arises from the fact that man is a spiritual being who has within him aspirations towards the infinite and the eternal, and that at the same time he is placed within the restricted conditions of existence in this world. Suffering which belongs to death, suffering which derives from love, from the conflict between love and political and religious convictions, from the enigmatic nature of life, from inability to comprehend one's own destiny, suffering which comes from an evil will to power and violence, suffering which arises from jealousy, from self-love, from envy, from the wounded feelings of a man who does not play the part which he would like to play, and from the lowering of his position in society, the suffering which arises from fear as man faces life and faces death, suffering which is due to meaningless chance accidents, to disillusionment about people, to the treachery of friends, to a melancholy temperament, and many other forms of suffering, all such are not removable by any sort of new social order. When the social problem has been solved and all men are settled in the conditions of a worthy existence, when there is no suffering which is due to a lack of guarantee of one's position in society, or to hunger, to cold, to illiteracy, to sickness, to injustice, then, precisely then, the feeling and consciousness of the insuperably tragic nature of life will be intensified. It is precisely then that an agonizing yearning will lay its hold upon not only the chosen few but upon the many. The social conflict with suffering gives an answer to the subject of suffering in general terms, but not to the suffering of concrete creatures. The laws of society may be a guarantee against social manifestations of cruelty, but they cannot destroy cruelty in the human heart, and that will always find forms which are not social for its expression. And in the same way the establishment of a social order with its guarantees of freedom for man and the citizen still will not deliver man from all possibility of slavery.

It does not, of course, follow from this that there is no need to make social changes of the most radical kind for the lessening of human suffering and human slavery. On the contrary everything ought to be done and the spiritual problems of man ought to be liberated from distorting social influences. The optimistic theory of progress which belonged to the nineteenth century was permeated by a belief in the possibility of abolishing suffering and in the progressive increase of happiness. This belief has been shattered by catastrophic world events. The old idea of progress is inadmissible. But there was Christian truth in it too. There was in it unperceived aspiration towards the Kingdom of God. The existence of an irrational principle in the life of the world has to be admitted, one which is not open to rationalization and belongs to no kind of progress. No sort of progress, no kind of social reconstruction can vanquish death, the chief source of suffering, or abolish the fear of the future. N. Fedorov understood this better than anyone else.[1]

Intensity of suffering is linked with intensity of life, with the expression of personality. To refuse intensity of life, and to refuse

[1] See N. Fedorov, *Philosophy of the Common Task.*

personality may be to mitigate pain. In that case man moves away from the world into himself, away from a world which is full of suffering and causes suffering to him, but in withdrawing into himself and isolating himself he begins to experience new sufferings, and to feel a need to go out from himself again, to escape from the torturing engulfment in self. The man who is suffering seeks to overcome his suffering, and find relief from it in various ways, and it is not always the case that he turns his attention to the highest, it is not always that this attempt of his bears witness to the high stature of man. Victory over suffering is sought by means of fusion with the social group, with the collective life; men try to find it by way of indifference or of apathy; it is sought through the regimentation of life or by submerging oneself in the humdrum, the trivial and banal. It is sought for in the forgetfulness of the moment. Men seek to conquer suffering by blunting the edge of consciousness, by a return to the sub-conscious, and it is but rarely that they seek relief and liberation in an uplifting impulse towards the supraconscious and superhuman. His own suffering is relieved when a man begins to experience sympathy with another. Most of all perhaps suffering is vanquished by contemplation of the Cross.

But man is so strange a creature that he not only seeks for liberation from suffering; he seeks out suffering also, and is ready to torture himself as he tortures others. Dostoyevsky understood this better than anyone. Even in the religious life, in its highest form, in the Christian life, men see not only the liberation from suffering which it promises to man, but also an intensification of suffering, the preaching of self-torture and the torture of others. There is in human beings a need to kill and torture for the sake of an idea and a faith. A new Christian consciousness ought to free man from these nightmares. It is not only external and physical tortures which are repulsive, but inward spiritual tortures also. It is above all a question of freeing the knowledge of God and the apprehension of God from the sadistic and vengeful instincts which have been transferred to Him. The most sadistic form of cruelty is to be seen among people who exercise power, any sort of power—religious, national, political, economic, or family, and it is provided with a basis in the realm of ideas. Power drives men mad, it is an endless longing desire. Some of the Roman emperors displayed the madness of cruelty. There are régimes which represent a crystallization of sadistic cruelty.

Man experiences suffering in very different ways according to whether he accepts it for the sake of his faith and his ideas, in which he will endure tortures; or whether he suffers from the ill-starred coincidence of circumstances and the senseless cruelty of the people who surround him and of the régime under which he lives. There is a difference between the suffering in which a man considers himself guilty, debased, vile, and suffering in which he heroically endures oppression and persecution. Suffering cannot be measured and compared, just as it is impossible to compare and measure joy and happiness. Suffering is experienced in different ways by women, by people of creative intellectual work, by those who belong to the simple folk, and so on. It is difficult for the present-day man, complex, subtlized and physically enfeebled to understand how it is possible to bear the suffering which a Protopope Avvakum or a Stenka Razin endured. Even in civilized man there remains from ancient days a thirst for blood, a longing for cruel spectacles, gladiatorial fights, bull fights and the rest. Mephistopheles says: '*Blut ist ein ganz besonderer Saft*'. There is an element of mystery in blood. The ancients located the soul in the blood; the cessation of life is also connected with it. Morally it was an immense step forward when the conviction of primitive people that the unfortunate were forsaken by the gods and ought to be shunned by men was overcome. Suffering is vanquished by love, but at the same time love may be a source of new suffering. I am not now speaking of eros love but of caritative love, love which is pity and sympathy.

It is very difficult for a man to go through suffering alone and in no way to give expression to it. Loneliness is one of the sources of suffering. In a certain sense it may be said that the creator is always lonely and always goes through suffering. The need to share one's suffering with others is expressed in complaint, tears and cries. In this way, so to speak, man asks for help. But there are reserved people who proudly bear their suffering inwardly, who try not to reveal it in any way. For that reason it should always be thought that people are very unhappy and that they are suffering, although we do not notice the fact. It might be well to behave to every man as though he were a dying man. There is nothing more painful than to see the vigour, bloom and joy of an exuberant life side by side with enfeeblement of life, with withering and the process of dying. But such is the fate of life, the fate of every developed individuality. Suffering and death are linked with love, which ought to conquer both suffering and death.

Happiness is not the conscious aim of human life, and I have already said that happiness cannot be organized. Blessedness may be thought of as the attainment of fullness of perfection, but that is not to be found upon earth. Here only separate moments of it are possible. But we can strive to lessen the amount of suffering and we ought to do so. Compassion is an absolute command. No-one ought to increase the amount of suffering for himself, to inflict suffering upon himself, but he ought to bear the suffering which may be sent from above with an enlightened mind as something which has a meaning in his destiny. The tormenting problem of suffering is not to be finally solved within the confines of this phenomenal world. The contradiction between the need of man and the conditions of his finite existence in the natural world is insoluble and presupposes the necessity of an act of transcendence, and of an end. Is it possible for the Good to save from suffering? It does not save and it cannot save and, therefore, redemption and a Redeemer are necessary; it is divine love and not only human which is needed. There is a powerlessness of man in the face of evil and suffering. But there is a powerlessness even of God Himself as Creating Power. Only God Who has become Man and taken upon Himself the suffering of man and of the whole creation can vanquish the source of evil which gives rise to suffering. No theological system and no authority can put an end to human suffering and torment. Only the primary realities of religion, only the divine-human link, only the divine-human love, can bring them to an end. Man, who is finally severing this divine-human link, stands facing the abyss of non-being and his suffering becomes unendurable.

All love brings new sufferings with it, and at the same time only love conquers suffering. It is divine-human love which conquers. Eros love has endless suffering in it; there is an element of insatiability in it. Love which is agape, the love which moves downward not upward, does not include infinite craving.[1] For this reason the two sorts of love ought to be combined, otherwise fullness is not attained. The creative power of man also conquers suffering, although creativeness knows sufferings of its own. The meaning of suffering is to be found where its cause is to be found. If, given the condition of disparity between the highest aspect of man's nature and the circumstances of his existence in this world, there were no suffering, man might sink into a wretched condition. And when all is said and done suffering remains a mystery to us. It is indeed the mystery of redemption.

The word redemption itself is too much associated with the very anthropomorphic and sociomorphic concept of ransom. To understand redemption as a ransom given to God in order to allay His wrath is degrading both to God and to man; it assumes that the sufferings of human beings and of the world are pleasing and acceptable to God. But a deeper and worthier conception is possible. Suffering is the testing of man, an assay of his spiritual strength as

[1] See Nygren, *Eros and Agape*, an interesting but arbitrary book.

he follows the paths of freedom. What is pleasing to God is not the man's suffering, but the transfiguration of his spiritual powers by the testing which suffering brings, by the inevitable results of freedom which is directed in a certain way, a freedom which in its origin is still pre-mundane. The stress must always be laid upon enlightenment and transfiguration.

CHAPTER VI

Evil

Suffering and evil are connected with each other, but they are not identical. Suffering may not be an evil; it may even be a good. The existence of evil is the greatest mystery in the life of the world and causes the greatest embarrassment to official theological doctrine and to all monistic philosophy. A rationalistic solution of the problem of evil is just as beset with difficulty as a solution of the problem of freedom. It can be asserted and with good grounds, that evil has no positive existence and that it can only allure by what it filches from good.[1] But none the less evil not only exists but it prevails in the world. What may be called non-being may have an existential significance; nonentity has great existential significance, although it would be untrue to say that it exists.[2] One of the attempts to solve the problem of evil, and to reconcile it with the possibility of theodicy, amounts to this, that evil is present only in the parts, whereas in the whole there is only good. It was thus that St Augustine thought, and Leibnitz, and indeed in the last resort, most forms of theodicy adopt the same position, for they admit that God uses evil for the purposes of good. But that sort of doctrine is based upon the denial of the unconditional significance of all personality, and it is a characteristic rather of ancient moral philosophy than of Christian. It means the prevalence of the æsthetic point of view over the ethical.

[1] St Gregory of Nyssa, St Augustine and other doctors of the Church considered that evil is non-being.

[2] Bergson in *Evolution Créatrice* rejects nonenity, non-being (*néant*), but his arguments are not convincing. Heidegger and Sartre assign great importance to it.

It is in fact true that in this empirical world there is no good divine teleological principle, and indeed there cannot be in a world which is recognized as fallen. It might be said that such exists for separate groups of phenomena but not for the whole phenomenal world, not as a connecting link among these phenomena for the sake of Good. The traditional doctrine of Providence is compelled to deny the evil and injustice of the world and it finds a way out of the difficulty in the fact that instead of evil it recognizes simply the existence of sin. There is in our world an insurmountable conflict between the individual and the race. The individual life, both human and animal, is fragile and menaced to an extraordinary degree, but at the same time our racial life has an extraordinary productive power, and is always begetting life afresh. The doctrine which sees evil only in the parts and does not see it in the whole, is at the mercy of race and is indifferent to the individual. The genius of race is cunning; it is always prompting unhappy man to accept false justifications, and by means of these it holds him in bondage; and historical and social life is, therefore, based upon an accumulation of such falsehood. A lie may be self-deception, when a man becomes the plaything of the commonplace social forces of life. A lie may also take the form of a defence of life against attacks upon it. The question of truth and falsehood is a fundamental moral question.

Man seeks to find refuge from the tormenting question of evil in the realm of neutrality, and by doing so seeks to conceal his treachery to God. But in the deeper sense there is no neutrality; the neutral is on the surface. It might even be said that the devil is neutral. It is a mistake to suppose that the devil is the polar opposite of God. The pole which is the direct opposite of God is again God, the other face of God; extremes meet. The devil is the prince of this world and he takes cover in neutrality. In religious life in general, and in the Christian life, belief in demons and in the devil has played an enormous rôle. It has been one of the solutions of the problem of evil. When the devil is regarded as the source of evil, objectivization of the interior drama of the human soul takes place. The devil is an existential reality but is certainly not an objective reality in the world of things like the realities of the natural world. He is a reality of spiritual experience, of the path along which man goes. The idea of the devil has been greatly abused socially. Men and women have been held in fear by it, and the kingdom of the devil has been expanded to enormous dimensions, new areas have been continually added to it. Thus a real spiritual reign of terror has been established. Liberation of the soul from the demons which torment it is possible only in a purified spiritual religion. Demonology and demonolatry have existed only on the path which man follows towards the kingdom of spirit, towards the kingdom of freedom and love, towards the Kingdom of God.

The fight against evil easily acquires an evil character itself; it becomes infected by evil. There is a sinister moral dialectic of Manichæan dualism. Too great foes of evil become evil themselves. This is a paradox of the conflict with evil and with evil men and things. The good become evil for the sake of victory over evil and do not believe in the use of other methods than evil in the conflict against evil. Kindliness invites an attitude of disdain, it appears to be uninteresting and insipid. Malice, on the other hand, imposes itself and appears more interesting and more attractive. Those engaged in the struggle think that malice is more intelligent than kindness. Here the problem lies in the fact that actually it is impossible to give effect to the purposes of good, to good ends; this too easily leads to evil and the employment of evil means. It is necessary to be within the good and to radiate the good. It is only the Gospel which overcomes this rebirth of the conflict with evil in the form of a new evil, and regards the condemnation of sinners as a new sin. One must behave with humanity and kindliness even to the devil. There is a dialectic of one's behaviour to the enemy and to evil. You begin by fighting in the name of good against the enemy, against the evil, but you end by being yourself permeated with evil. The problem of one's attitude to the enemy is the fundamental moral problem of our time. The enemy is ceasing to be regarded as a man, there must be no human attitude towards him. In this respect the greatest apostasy from the truth of the Gospel has taken place. I do not think that there are any hopelessly demoniacal natures, that is to say natures over whom the doom of demoniacal possession hangs, just as I do not think that demoniacal nations have existed. What exists is simply a demoniacal condition of people and nations and, therefore, a final judgment is possible upon nobody.

As there is a dialectic of the attitude to the enemy in virtue of which he who fights an evil enemy in the name of good becomes evil, so also there is a dialectic of humility in virtue of which it is turned into passivity in the face of evil, and into accommodation to evil. In the same way there is a dialectic of punishment for crime which turns the punishment itself into a crime. There is in human beings an irresistible need for a scapegoat, for an enemy who is to blame for all their misfortunes and whom they can and even should hate. It may be the Jews, heretics, masons, Jesuits, Jacobins, Bolshevists, bourgeois, international secret societies, and so forth. Revolution always requires an enemy for its nourishment and if there is no enemy it invents one. The same is true of counter-revolution. When the scapegoat is found man begins to feel better. This is an objectivization of evil, an ejection of it into external reality. The State rightly carries on a fight against crime, and against external expressions of evil which are unduly vigorous, but nevertheless the State itself commits crime and does evil. As 'the most cold-blooded of monsters' (the expression is Nietzche's) it commits crime, it creates evil without passion and in the abstract. In upholding law and right the State defends the good but it creates its own particular evil. The evil need to experience he joy of cruelty is objectivized, the collective sense of satisfaction in being the cause of pain, in having the right to punish and to be present at the infliction of punishment.

The relations between good and evil are not simple and there is a complex existential dialectic in them. Good may be reborn as evil and evil may be reborn as good. The very distinction between good and evil has been an unhealthy and morbid division and has borne the impress of having passed through the Fall.[1] There is something servile in the interpretation of sin as crime which infringes the will of God and calls for legal proceedings on the part of God. To overcome this servile conception means movement within, movement in depth. Sin is dividedness, a state of deficiency, incompleteness, dissociation, enslavement, hatred, but it is not disobedience and not formal violation of the will of God. It is impossible and inadmissible to construct an ontology of evil. The idea of an eternal hell is, therefore, absurd and evil. Evil is but a pathway, a testing, a disruption; to fall into sin is above all else a testing of freedom. Man moves towards the light through the darkness. Dostoyevsky revealed this more profoundly than anyone.

Evil is usually explained in terms of freedom. This is the most widespread explanation of evil. But freedom is a mystery which does not lend itself to rationalization. The traditional doctrine of the schools about the freedom of the will is static and reveals very little of the mystery of the rise of evil. It remains incomprehensible how out of the good nature of man and of the devil himself, out of heavenly life in the rays of the light of God, there could arise—thanks to the freedom of the creature (freedom which it understood to be the highest gift of God and a mark of likeness to God)—how there could arise evil and the evil life of man and of the world, evil which is reminiscent of hell. It is necessary to concede the existence of an uncreated freedom which precedes being

[1] See my book, *The Destiny of Man*.

and is submerged in the irrational sphere, in what Boehme calls the *Ungrund*, though he gave a somewhat different meaning to it. The recognition of such a freedom, preceding being, preceding creation, premundane, sets before man the creative task of continuing the creation of the world, and makes evil itself a path, a grievous experience, but not an ontological principle which passes over into eternity (hell). Freedom must be understood dynamically, as engaged in a dialectic process. There are contradictions in freedom, and varying conditions and laws belong to it. Evil raises the eschatological problem in an acute form and it is removed and overcome only eschatologically.

The fight against evil must be carried on and evil must be finally overcome, and at the same time the experience of evil has been a path which leads not only downwards but upwards also. It is not evil itself which has been an upward path, but the spiritual strength of the resistance aroused by it and the knowledge which was born of it. Evil is meaningless, and at the same time it has the highest meaning. In the same way freedom is the antithesis of necessity and bondage, but it can be reborn as necessity and bondage, it can pass into its opposite. Man must go through the testing of all possibilities, he must pass through the experience of the knowledge of good and evil, and evil itself may become a dialectic moment of good. And evil must be overcome immanently, that is to say. there must take place what Hegel called *Aufhebung*, when the negative is overcome, and all the positive enters into the subsequent stage. Thus even atheism may become a dialectic moment in the knowledge of God. It is the lot of man to pass through atheism, through communism, and many other such things in order that he may move out towards the light by an immanent, enriching, act of overcoming. What is needed is not the destruction of those who are 'evil' but their enlightenment. Evil can be vanquished only from within, not by violent prohibition alone, nor can it be destroyed by force. Yet at the same time external limits ought to be set to the manifestations of evil which are destructive of life. Both a spiritual and a social conflict ought to be carried on against evil, and the social conflict cannot avoid having recourse to force in the conditions of this world. But the spiritual conflict, on the other hand, can only be carried on as a process of enlightenment and transfiguration, not by resort to violence.

The experience of evil cannot in itself enrich, if one surrenders to it. It is only that positive radiant spiritual power which is brought out in the overcoming of evil, which is able to enrich. Light presupposes darkness, good presupposes evil, creative development presupposes not only 'this' but also 'the other'. It was Boehme and Hegel who understood this best. Evil has the mastery in this world, but it is not to evil that the last word belongs. Evil can be a dialectic moment in the unfolding development of created things, but only because through it the good which is opposed to it is disclosed. The idea of hell and the torments of hell was an eternalization of evil; it represents a failure of strength in the face of it. Evil presupposes freedom and there is no freedom without the freedom of evil, that is to say there is no freedom in a state of compulsory good. But evil is directed against freedom; it seeks to destroy it and to enthrone slavery. According to Kierkegaard man becomes an ego through sin; only he who goes down into hell knows heaven, and he who is the farther from God may be the nearer to God. In Kierkegaard's view the begetting of children is the primary sin. Baader says that life is born in pain and makes its appearance only after a descent into hell. There is a flash of light on the frontier between the world of darkness and the world of light. At the outset evil behaves towards us as towards a master, later on it treats us as fellow-workers and in the end itself becomes the master. All ideas are dynamic, they presuppose contradiction and a process which arises from contradiction.

Two opposite causes give rise to evil in man. Either a vacuum is formed in the soul and proves attractive to evil, or a passion which has become an *idée fixe*, and crowded out everything else, degenerates into evil. Such passions are, for instance, ambition, avarice, jealousy, hatred. The passion is not yet evil in itself but it easily becomes an evil and leads to the loss of inward freedom. A passion for death is also possible.[1] It is difficult for a man in whom moral and religious consciousness has been already formed to commit the first transgression, but the first offence easily gives rise to the second offence, and the man enters into a magical atmosphere of delinquency. This is admirably depicted by Shakespeare in Macbeth. It is difficult to enter upon the path of terrorism, but afterwards it is difficult to stop and bring it to an end. Evil is above all the loss of integrality; it is a breaking away from the spiritual centre, and the formation of autonomous parts which begin to carry on an independent existence of their own. The good in man, on the other hand, is inner integrality, interior unity, the subordination of the life of the soul and of bodily life to a spiritual principle. Evil belongs to this world and, given an apophatic interpretation of the divine, it cannot be transferred to the life beyond. The idea of hell was not a victory over evil but rather an immortalization of it.

In the face of the tormenting problem of evil, both optimism and pessimism are alike untrue. What is needed is to be more of a pessimist in the recognition of evil in this phenomenal world where the prince of this world reigns, and more of an optimist in the denial of it in the world beyond. The concrete knowledge of life, the vision of all its secrets in detail, is a very bitter knowledge. The coming of a better life is merely symbolized in revolutions, political or religious, the better life itself does not come, the en-

[1] Ribault defines passion as a protracted and intellectualized emotion. It must be said that an emotion does not exist in a pure isolated aspect; the whole man is always present also, even if in a tormented state, and there is an intellectual element in the most mad and most irrational condition of man.

tirely new man does not make his appearance. Always the very basest expressions of human life come to light anew; in oppression and persecution, whether it be religious, national, or political, whether it be the outcome of class feeling or belongs to the realm of ideas. Collective enthusiasm easily ends in the setting up of a Gestapo or a Cheka. The life of man in civilization has an irresistible tendency to disintegration, corruption, to collapse into fatuity. Then appears the desire to save oneself by movement in the opposite direction, to take refuge in nature, in the country, in labour, asceticism, monasticism; but this movement also easily leads to ossification or to dissolution.

It is an astounding thing that when people repent they do not, as a rule, repent for that for which they needed to repent. Torquemada did not repent of his actual sin as an inquisitor, he was convinced that he was serving God. Christian people desire not so much a real change and transformation of their nature as absolution for their sins. Religious ideologies and beliefs become a matter of fresh hatred and hostility. The religion of love and forgiveness enshrines a struggle for power. States and societies are always offensive and aggressive, so that human personality is obliged to be always on the defensive. The love of woman may have a redemptive saving significance (in *The Flying Dutchman*; in the case of Sollweg in *Peer Gynt*; or Jouhandot in *Véronique*). Here the image of the Mother of God is, as it were, always meeting us. But the love of woman can much more often be a cause of ruin. Propitiatory blood sacrifices should have had a redemptive significance, but, as it was, they expressed the cruelty and bloodthirstiness of man. And to this very day bloody human sacrifices are offered for the sake of ideas and beliefs which have all the appearance of nobility. All this bitter knowledge of life is not final knowledge, it is not knowledge of the last things. Behind all the darkness of the world and human life a light is hidden, and there are other moments when this light is so strong that it blinds us. Man ought to look evil straight in the face, to allow himself no illusions about it, but never to be overwhelmed by it. Truth lies beyond optimism and pessimism. The absurdity of the world is not a denial of the existence of meaning. The exposure of lack of meaning presupposes the existence of meaning. The evil of the world presupposes the existence of God, without it it would be impossible to get to know Him.

Nobility, the quality which I call true aristocracy, requires of a man the recognition of his guilt. In its depths, conscience, which is frequently covered up and suppressed, is always a consciousness of guilt. The necessary thing is to take upon oneself as much guilt as possible and to put as little as possible of it upon other people. The aristocrat is not one who is proudly conscious of himself as first, as a privileged being, and who safeguards his position as such. The aristocrat is the man who is aware of the guilt and sinfulness of this first place, this privileged position of his. The sense that one is being continually affronted is on the other hand, precisely a plebian feeling. But it is all too easy to condemn the *ressentiment* of the oppressed and those whose position in society comes last. Max Scheler has done this, and most unjustly, from the point of view of a Nietzscheanized Christianity.[1] The *ressentiment*, into which envy enters is indisputably not a noble sentiment, but there may be all too good grounds for its existence, and it is not for him who is to blame for the *ressentiment* of the humiliated, to busy himself with accusations of it. None the less the most profound thing is not the consciousness of one's own sinfulness (which may remain in the sphere of psychology and ethics), but the metaphysical consciousness of the position of man in the world; man who has infinite struggling aspirations while placed in the circumstances of a finite and compressed existence. In this lies the fall of man, and in this lies the origin of the formation by unenlightened passions of illusory false worlds.

[1] See Max Scheler, *L'Homme de Ressentiment.*

Man finds difficulty in enduring the fact that he is in this world as a mortal creature and that everything which happens in him and with him is mortal. Hence the problem of evil is above all the problem of death. Victory over evil is victory over death. Evil is death; victory over evil is the resuscitation of life, rebirth to a new life. Murder, hatred, revenge, treachery and perfidy, debauchery, slavery, are death. The victory of God-manhood over the last enemy, death, is victory over evil. It is the victory of love, of freedom and creativeness, over hatred, slavery and inertia, the victory of personality over impersonality. The last enemy, death, has a positive meaning too. The tragic sense of death is connected with an acute sense of personality, of personal destiny. For the life of the race there is nothing tragic in death. The life of the race always renews itself and continues, it finds compensation for itself. Death appals the most developed and individualized organism most of all. With an acute sense of personality is associated an acute sense of evil also. The positive meaning of death lies in the fact that its inevitability for the individual personal existence is evidence of the unattainability of the infinite enterprizes of life, and of the impossibility of realizing fullness of life within the limits of this world and this time.[1]

Death, that final evil, is one of the paths to eternity. Endless life in the conditions of our limited existence would be a nightmare. To pass through death is just as necessary for our personal destiny in eternity, as the end of the world is necessary for the accomplishment of its eternal destiny. The antinomies and problems of human life and of the life of the world are insoluble in this æon, and, therefore, a transition to another æon is necessary. For this reason fear of death is not the only possibility; there is also an attraction of death. The thought of death is sometimes a consolation to a man when the contradictions of his life become intolerable, when the evil around him grows too dense. Freud regarded the instinct

[1] See my book, *The Destiny of Man.*

of death not only as of a higher order than the sexual instinct but as the sole elevated instinct in man.[1] Heidegger is likewise compelled to recognize death as higher than *Dasein*, which is submerged in the humdrum and prosaic, in *das Man*.[2] The last word in his philosophy belongs to death. It is an interesting fact that to the German spirit there is in general something attractive about death, victory and death. Wagner's music was permeated with the sense of victory and death; Nietzsche preached the will to power and an ecstatic joy in life, but in his perpetually tragic feeling about life the most profound and final thing was *Amor fati*. There has been depth in the German spirit but there has been no resuscitating strength.

That resuscitating strength does exist in the Russian spirit, and Fedorov represented the summit of its expression. And it is not a matter of chance that the principal festival of Russian Orthodoxy is the Feast of the Resurrection of Christ. It is thus that Christianity is understood. The source of victory over the evil of life in this world is not in death and it is not in birth, but in resurrection. The experience of the evil of the world destroys, but the creative power of resurrection conquers evil and death. Christian ethics in respect of evil as a whole and of individual evils can but be paradoxical. In Christ the God-Man and in the divine-human process, the transfiguration of the whole cosmos is being made ready. It is impossible to think of evil and of freedom, which is connected with evil, in an ontological and static way. They must be thought of dynamically in the language of spiritually existential experience.

[1] See Freud, *Essais de Psychologie*.
[2] See Heidegger, *Sein und Zeit*.

CHAPTER VII

War

War is a basic fact of our world era. It is a fact not only of the social and historical life of man, but also of cosmic life. Heraclitus said that war has a universal character and that everything is destroyed as the result of dissension. The cosmic character of war in his opinion is a result of the fact that the world is movement and is embraced by fire. Hobbes maintained that the primitive state was one of war. War exists not only upon earth but also in heaven; the angels and demons wage war. The history of the world has to a very large extent consisted of war; it has been a history of wars. Short periods of peace, for example the last quarter of the nineteenth century, have given the false impression that peace and not war is the normal thing in history. The outlook of the humanists in the nineteenth century was in this respect false.

War is waged between peoples, between families, between classes and estates. There are wars within social groups and political parties, wars between nations and states. Finally there is among men no less an inclination to wars of religion and ideological wars. In fact there has never been a stabilized order; there has always been war, an internal state of war. War is the final expression of every way of realizing one's end by means of force. And every man who is permeated by an integral idea which he desires at whatever cost to realize, for example to assure a dominating position for the Christian Church, to create a great empire, to bring about a great revolution, to win a war, may indeed display heroism; but he may also easily turn not only into a man of violence but even into a wild beast. War takes place because there is 'this' and there is 'the other', because every course of action meets with opposition, because contradiction is of the essence of the life of the world. Human beings cannot live in harmony with one another; they cannot live in harmony in any group whether in a family, or in some economic, political, social, religious or ideological association. For two friends, or two lovers, for parents and children, for two people who hold the same beliefs, two of the same way of thinking, transition to a state of war is easy. Egoism, self-assertion, envy, jealousy, self-love, self-interest and fanaticism, readily lead to war.

There is an existential dialectic of union and division. People preach the brotherhood of man, but there can be no brotherly union between those who uphold the brotherhood of man and of peoples, and those who oppose it; and the advocates of brotherhood resort to war against the opponents of brotherhood. People preach freedom, but in regard to dangerous opponents of freedom they are obliged to resort to force and to deny them their freedom. People strive against evil in the name of good, and then begin to create evil by their attitude towards the representatives of evil. People and nations may be permeated by the pacific idea of abolishing war, but for the sake of that idea they are driven to declare war upon those who uphold war. A vicious circle is the result. The psychology of fanaticism, of a fanatical and exclusive adherence to some idea or other, religious, national, political, social, inevitably leads to war. To act is to meet with contrary action, to quarrel, and in the last resort to wage war. There is in men a deep-seated need to quarrel; there are warlike instincts which are not to be uprooted. The Indians, who are most peaceful people, justified war and killing in war[1] in their religious poem the *Bhagavad-gita*. War creates its own types of society and every state adopts the symbolism of war. In war human blood flows abundantly. But the shedding of blood has a quite peculiar and mysterious significance.

[1] *La Bhagavad-gita, interprétée par Shri Aurobindo.*

The shedding of blood envenoms whole peoples and gives rise to ever more and more bloodshed. Although they recognize murder as a sin and a crime, people are none the less fond of idealizing certain forms of murder—the duel, war, capital punishment, the disguised murder of political persecution; and blood always begets blood. 'They that take the sword shall perish with the sword.' The shedding of blood cannot fail to arouse alarm and consternation. In ancient orgiastic cults blood and sex were associated;[1] and this mysterious link does exist. The shedding of blood regenerates human beings.

The difficulty of solving the problem of war is due to its twofold nature. On the one hand war is a zoological stage in the development of mankind; it is a sin and an evil. On the other hand wars have provided a way of escape from the humiliating prosiness of every day; they have lifted men up above the pettiness of life. War has provided men with the possibility of performing heroic feats; it has demanded from them courage, fortitude, sacrifice, loyalty and the refusal of safety. And yet again war has unbridled the very lowest instincts of man—cruelty, bloodthirstiness, violence, rapine, and the will to power.[2] Heroism itself can be negative as well as positive. The seductive lure of military glory is anti-Christian in character. The demand for the deification of Caesars, generals, leaders, for the deification of antichrists, is connected with war. This must be distinguished from the reverence paid to geniuses and saints. Two fates lie in wait for man, either war, violence, blood and heroism which merge into the seductive lie of majestic greatness, or pettiness, complacency, the enjoyment of life, and the power of money. Men and peoples oscillate between these two conditions and with difficulty attain a third and higher state.

War—I am talking about real war as we know it—is an extreme

[1] See Vyacheslav Ivanov, *The Religion of Dionysus*.

[2] On the twofold nature of war there are some remarkable thoughts in Proudhon. See his *La Guerre et la Paix*.

form of the domination of society over the person. This may be expressed in another way by saying that it is a manifestation of the hypnotic power of the collective over personality. Men can wage war only under conditions in which personal consciousness is enfeebled and group consciousness, collective consciousness, is strengthened. The development and the perfecting of the means of waging war are always greater than its objectivization.[1] The process of perfecting the technical side of war leads to this, that it moves ever further and further away from the warfare of chivalry in which the principle of individual personal valour and honour was strong. It was the use of fire-arms which began the destruction of knightly warfare. Earlier wars, which were waged by professional armies were localized; they did not involve whole countries and peoples. But the perfecting and the objectivization of war have made it totalitarian; there is no shelter from it anywhere. The highly complex art of war is, nevertheless, the art of killing people.[2] War is a great evil or rather it is the outward manifestation of an evil which has been seething in the depths of the external world. But total war is becoming a total evil.

The exposure of the great evil and sin of war ought not to lead to abstract pacifism in all circumstances. Given the evil of the state of our world, war may be a less evil. If aggressive and enslaving war is an absolute evil, defensive war or a war for liberation may be not only justified but even holy. The same must be said of revolution which is a form of war. Revolution is always cruel but it may be a blessing too. Patience is a virtue but it may turn into a vice and connive at evil. Good operates in the concrete world environment which is complex and dark, and the action of good cannot take place along a straight line. Good is compelled sometimes to try to attain what is the least evil. The final discontinu-

[1] See Ullrich, *La Guerre à Travers les Ages*.

[2] I had already finished this book when the atom bomb was invented. This marks a grave moment in the fatal dialectic of war.

ance of war is bound up with a change in the spiritual condition of human societies and of the social order. The capitalist order inevitably gives rise to war. To overcome war means to overcome the sovereignty of the State, and of nationalism; but to overcome the wars of revolution requires a radical social reformation of human societies.

To justify war and even to be enthusiastic about it, and at the same time to deny that revolution may be justified and permissible is to be guilty of a lie. Blood is shed in revolutions; but still more blood is shed in wars. Revolution is always accompanied by horrors but it may be a less evil than endless patience with slavery. Thus small revolutions are sometimes necessary within a family or in a State institution or in a public or an economic establishment. War and revolution are a judgment on people and nations who live in a condition of the severance of the divine-human links, in isolation not only from the human in general, but also from various separate parts of the human. Proudhon thought that war would be overcome when it is turned into revolution. But it is, none the less, utopian to think that the question of the structure of human societies can be solved apart from a profound change of spirit in man. War always brings barbarization with it; there is a conflict between a flourishing culture and military power. Thus, for example, more cultured peoples are being crowded out by the Turks. In the ancient world the Assyrians, who were the most warlike and the most barbarous of peoples, conquered them all. There is no ground for optimistically connecting might in this world with right, although the waging of war to win freedom and in defence of truth may be associated with real spiritual exaltation and may reveal the strength of truth and right.

The only pacifist who has been thoroughly consistent is Leo Tolstoy. His doctrine of non-resistance to evil by force, his repudiation of the laws of this world in the name of the law of God, goes deeper than is supposed; he has been badly misunderstood. Tolstoy confronted a Christian world which had become habituated to its own lying, with this problem: Is it possible to attain happiness on earth by heavenly means? May spirit, even in the name of spirit, use force and violence? Is there a divine principle in man which is stronger than all the violence perpetrated by man? Is it possible to govern the human masses by divine truth? Tolstoy was a great awakener of the sleeping conscience. He demanded that people who believe in God should live and act in a different way from those who do not believe in God. What hurt him was that Christians, people who believe in God, live and arrange their affairs on earth as though there were no God, as though there had never been a Sermon on the Mount. Christians and non-Christians alike live by the law of the world and not by the law of God. But the law of the world is war, and the use of force by man upon man. Tolstoy believed that if men cease to oppose evil by force, which is also evil, there will be an immediate intervention of God and the good will conquer. Human resistance by the use of force hinders the operation of God in men. One may describe this point of view as quietistic mysticism applied to history and public life. There was much critical truth in Tolstoy but the root of his mistake is the fact that he does not understand the mystery of divine-humanity, that is of the two natures, distinct but united. He was a monist and his position was nearer to Indian religious philosophy and Buddhism than to Christian religious philosophy. He exposed and attacked the evils of historical life with enormous power, but he had no sense of metaphysical evil. He was right in thinking that it is impossible to overcome the evil in man by force. But the object of his exclusive interest was the man who uses force in the struggle against evil and the evil person; while he seemed to take no interest whatever in the fate of the man upon whom the evil men use force, and whom one ought to protect, and thus keep the external expression of evil within bounds. And so, in his view, a defensive war, or a war of liberation, is no different from an aggressive and enslaving war. Tolstoy wants the law of God to reign, not the law of the world; the law of love, and not the law of force; in this he expressed a sacred truth. But how is this to be attained? The final triumph of what he calls the law of the Householder of Life means the transformation of the world, it means the end of this world, of this earth, and the beginning of a new world and a new earth. But Tolstoy remains a great awakener for Christians.

The metaphsycial problem of war is the problem of the part played by force in the conditions of this phenomenal world. When Tolstoy teaches that God is not in power but in truth and right, he is setting a Russian idea in antithesis to a German idea: he is opposing both Hegel and Nietzsche. The real greatness of Tolstoy lay in his exposure of wrong and the utter insignificance of every sort of greatness which belongs to this world. Every form of the greatness of the world is paltry and wretched;—the greatness of kingly power, of illustrious birth, military greatness or the greatness of wealth and luxury, the greatness of Julius Caesar and of Napoleon. It is the greatness of a fallen phenomenal world which has not risen to noumenal significance. Historical greatness is too much associated with falsehood, malice, cruelty, violence and blood. The 'great' historic events are a stage-show behind which an entirely different reality is concealed. The love of the human masses and their leaders for ceremonies, for conventional symbols, for orders, and uniforms, for high-flown rhetoric and for the useful lie, is evidence of the state of the world and of man in the world, and teaches us how necessary it is to govern the world with a lie. Not only Tolstoy's religious and moral treatises, but *War and Peace* also are full of exposures of the falsehood of this world, the falsehood of history and civilization.[1] There is no stronger evidence of the degradation of man than the difficulty

[1] The best book of a religious and philosophical character by Tolstoy is *Concerning Life*.

he finds in standing the test of victory. Man has discovered in himself heroic strength to bear persecution, but he has not been able to bear victory. After victory he sinks to a low level, he becomes violent and takes to persecution. Christians who were spiritual athletes in time of persecution, themselves became persecutors after they had won the victory. There is no greater test than the test which victory brings, and one might say, 'Woe to the victors in this world.' There is a paradox in the dialectic of power and victory. Victory presupposes power, but it is moral power. But victory easily reincarnates power in the form of coercive force and destroys its moral character. All this leads to the central problem of the relation between the spirit and power.

The overwhelming majority of people, including Christians, are materialists; they do not believe in the power of spirit; they believe only in material power, military or economic power; and it is futile for them to wax indignant against the Marxists. The very antithesis of spirit and power is conventional and inaccurate. The concept of power has many meanings. People derive it from the experience of muscular effort and of the capacity of the will to realize so and so. But the philosophy of power is naturalistic metaphysics. The philosophy of life is also naturalistic and leads to the apotheosis of power. The naturalistic conception of power has been transferred to social life also and even to ecclesiastical life. The Church has constantly had recourse to the power of the State, that is to say to material power. One can, however, speak not only of material power, but of spiritual power also. Christ spoke as one having authority, that is, He spoke with power. This was power of another kind. We speak of the power of love, the power of spirit, the power of great spiritual achievements, the power of sacrifice, the power of knowledge, the power of moral conscience, the power of creative impulse. We speak of the power of truth, the power of freedom, the power of a miracle which has overthrown the dominion of the power of nature.

The true antithesis is between power and coercive force. But here too the antithesis is more complex than is commonly thought. In addition to obvious physical force which leaps to the eye, there is also the less noticed psychological force to which people are constantly exposed. This sort of coercive force may be even more horrible than physical violence. There is in this connection a complex scale of degrees of violence. One's upbringing, religious fear, family manners, propaganda, the daily suggestion of the newspaper, the dominance of political parties, the power of money, all these may be forms of coercive force, and there are many others. Man is exposed to violence not only through bodily acts but also through actions which work upon his mind and hold him in the grip of fear. A régime based upon terror is not only a matter of actions in the material sphere, of arrests, tortures, and executions, it is above all something which works upon the human mind and spirit; it is the inspiring of fears and the keeping of people in a state of fear. Thus terrible force of this kind was exerted upon men in the Middle Ages through fear of the pains of hell. There is always this sort of coercive force when interior freedom has no part in the influence which is exercised. Power in the bad sense is always associated with the denial of another's freedom. The man of violence likes freedom for himself but denies it to others. The upholders of despotic régimes always like freedom for themselves; they allow themselves much too much freedom of movement; it would be better to set bounds to it.

Power in itself is not a value; in itself it is not a good. The higher values are in this world weaker than the lower values; spiritual values are not so strong as material.[1] The prophet, the philosopher or the poet is less strong than the policeman or the soldier. The greatest power of all in this fallen empirical world is the power of money and the power of big guns. The greatest spiritual values

[1] There are some interesting thoughts on this subject in N. Hartmann, *Das Problem des geistigen Seins*.

can be destroyed by the guns. The Roman soldiers were stronger than the Son of God. Therefore the worship of power as power is godless and inhuman. The cult of power is the cult of the lower material power; it shows disbelief in the power of spirit and in the power of freedom. But obviously the antithesis of the false worship is not the defence of feebleness and impotence, it is spirit and freedom, and in social life, right and justice. The law of this natural phenomenal world is the struggle of individuals, families, class, tribes, nations and states and empires for existence and dominance. This is the law of war. The demon of the will to power torments men and peoples. But into this terrible world the principle of spirit, freedom, humanity, and mercy can force its way. Christ was against those who are 'first', that is to say the strong. Christianity is in truth radically opposed to the worship of power. It is against natural selection. The cult of power is not a Russian cult.

War poses the even sharper question of one's relation to the enemy. The dialectic of war leads to this, that the enemy ceases to be considered as a human being, and so far as he is concerned everything is permissible. Chivalry required chivalrous behaviour even to the enemy, and this attitude held its ground for a long while. The enemy was buried with military honours. But war has ceased to be chivalrous and precisely because it has become total. Cruelty is permitted and encouraged in regard to the enemy. If cruelty is practised upon one's friends and neighbours they become one's foes. The dialectic of war which is completely transforming it and imparting to it progressively less and less of any human character, is due to the extraordinary development of the technical side of war. Destruction and slaughter which are monstrous in scale and directed against whole peoples will lead in the last resort to the self-negation of war. As a result of new weapons, poison gas and the atomic bomb, war is being transformed into a new thing for which there is as yet no name. Weapons of destruction are so terrible when they fall into the hands of evil men who have power to use them, that the question of the spiritual state of human societies is raised in a peculiarly acute form. The romantic idealization of war is bound up with the cult of heroism and of heroes. This corresponds with something which lies very deep in human nature. But hero worship is an ancient Graeco-Roman cult. It was reborn in the Christian world as chivalry. In bourgeois civilization chivalry disappears, but majestic greatness continues to be associated with war. The last world war did indeed reveal extraordinary heroism side by side with extraordinary brutality, but the limits which the knightly mind marked out in respect of behaviour to the enemy were violated. Transfigured Christian heroism had very little chance of showing itself.

Fedorov believed in the possibility of bringing war to an end, and of directing the ineradicable fighting instincts of man into another sphere of life, into a struggle against the elemental forces of nature. This is evidence of the lofty moral thought of Fedorov, but at the same time it reveals his under-estimation of the power of evil in man and the world. War, I repeat, is an evil but it is not always the very greatest evil; it is sometimes a less evil as for instance when it brings liberation from the greatest of evils. War as a world phenomenon exists because there is an insufficiency of spiritual power. Men do not believe in the power of spirit; they believe only in the spirit of power. Instead of seeing their goal in spiritual life and culture they see it in the State and in the increase of its might. The ends of life are replaced by its means. This substitution of the means for the ends in life, this turning of means into self-sufficient purposes, is in its results one of the most serious and distressing processes in history. It always means the depreciation of spirit. To bow before power is false optimism, false monism. The shout of the conqueror which has resounded in the world has all too often been a sign that the world is lying in evil. Permission for the powerful to shed blood does not issue from God, it indicates rather a breach with God. This world remains far too indifferent to the fact that truth is crucified. The reign of war, the dominion of military strength in the world is an expression of disbelief in the power of the very truth itself, in the power of spirit and in the power of God. If spirit is power and the greatest power, it is power in a different sense from that which is honoured in the world. It is the power which might remove mountains. The break-through of spirit is possible in the world and it is by these manifestations that man has been kept alive and by which history has moved towards a super-historical end, towards the Kingdom of God.

Is the victory of the human possible in the conditions of our world? True humanity ought to assert itself even in the terrible circumstances of war. But its final victory is an issue which lies beyond the confines of this world. War in all its manifestations is an outcome of the severance of the divine-human link, of the godless autonomy of self-asserting power in the world and in men. Victory over the evil of war, and victory over evil in general, alike presuppose a radical change in human consciousness, they assume the overcoming of objectivization as a false orientation of consciousness. The enemy is one who is in the highest degree turned into an object, that is to say, existentially he is dissociated and insulated from us to the utmost. You can fight with the object only; to fight with the subject is impossible. But we live in a world of objectivization, in a world of dissociation, and it is for that reason that war holds dominion in it. The world of true humanity, of spirituality, of beauty and of immortality, is a different world from the world of fear and suffering, of evil and war upon which I have been dwelling.

CHAPTER VIII

Manhood

There does not exist as yet a real religious and metaphysical anthropology. Neither the anthropology of the Fathers, nor scholastic anthropology, nor yet the anthropology of the humanists, can satisfy us. The traditional Christian doctrine of man has not revealed the creative nature of man; it has been overwhelmed by the depressing consciousness of sin. On the other hand the conception of manhood has not gone right down into the depths of its metaphysical and religious foundations. True human-ness is likeness to God; it is the divine in man. The divine in man is not 'the super-natural' and it is not a special act of grace; it is a spiritual principle which is in man as a particular reality.[1] In this lies the paradox of the relations between the human and the divine. In order to be completely like man it is necessary to be like God. It is necessary to have the divine image in order to have the human image. Man as we know him is to but a small extent human; he is even inhuman. It is not man who is human but God. It is God Who requires of man that he should be human; man on his part makes very little demand for it. In exactly the same way it is God Who demands that man should be free, and not man himself. Man himself loves servitude and easily comes to terms with it. Freedom is not a right of man but a duty of man before God. And the same must be said about manhood. In realizing the image of God in himself man realizes the human image, and in

[1] In this respect I agree with S. Bulgakov, in spite of the fact that he differs greatly from me in the doctrine of freedom, creativeness and evil. See the last volume of his theological system, *The Bride of the Lamb*, which I read after my book was written. There are native traits of Russian religious philosophy which distinguish it from Christian thought in the West.

realizing in himself the human image he realizes the divine image. In this lies the mystery of God-manhood, the greatest mystery of human life. Manhood is God-manhood. Man realizes in himself the image of a beast much more than the image of God. Brute-manhood occupies an immeasurably greater place than God-manhood.

The image of the brute in man certainly does not mean likeness to the beast, which is a beautiful creation of God. What is horrible is not the beast but the man who has become a beast. A beast is immeasurably better than a man who has become its like. The beast never falls to such a dreadful level as that which man reaches. In a beast there is a likeness to the angels; it bears within it a distorted image of an angel in the same way as man bears within him the distorted image of God. But there is never in the beast such a dreadful distortion of its image as there is in man. The man is answerable for his condition of a beast in this world, whereas a beast is not responsible; and this is determined by the fact that man is a microcosm and possesses freedom which other parts of the cosmos do not possess to such a degree. If there is no God, man is a perfected, and at the same time a deteriorated, animal. God-manhood is a double mystery, a mystery of the birth of God in man and of man in God. There is not only man's need of God but also God's need of man. Monism, monophysism, denies the double truth and denies the independence of man. There are two movements, the movement from God towards man, and the movement from man towards God. Man is necessary for the divine life, for its fullness; and on that account only does the divine and human drama exist. The relations between God and man are not forensic but dramatic.

The birth of man in God is a theogonic process. In the eternal idea of him, man is rooted in God-manhood and linked with the God-man, and, therefore, it may be said that a pre-eternal manhood exists in God. The pre-eternal Man exists, whom the Kabbalah called the heavenly Adam. Humanity exists in eternity and ought to be realized in time. This is a mystery of the paradoxical relation between eternity and time. Eternity itself must be understood dynamically, not statically; in it absolute rest coincides with absolute movement. Humanness is not what is called humanism or humanitarianism, it is the God-manhood of man. Christological dogma expresses the truth about God-manhood symbolically, but it has not yet extended this truth to the whole of man, simply because he is man, that is to say a potential God-man. This cannot be comprehended in rational terms. If we conceive it in rational terms we always tend to deviate on the one hand to monism or on the other to dualism. It is very easy to give a rational exposition in the spirit of monism of the truth that the image of man is the image of God. But there is here the mystery of a union of two in one, of God-manhood, of a double movement. Of the doctors of the Church perhaps St Gregory of Nyssa alone defended the freedom and dignity of man as the image of God.[1] His anthropology is the best there has been in Christian thought about man.

Our understanding of man in general and of any concrete man in particular is very much confused by the fact that the composition of man is complex and it is not an easy matter to reduce the complexity to a unity. Personality in man is the result of conflict. It is the multiple composition of man that made possible those ancient conceptions which admitted the existence of a shadow, of a double of man; and it was difficult to decide which was the principal reality. There is no doubt a double ego in man—the true, the real, the deep ego, and the ego which is created by the imagination and passions, which is fictitious and which drags man downwards. Personality is worked out by a long drawn out process, by choice, by the crowding out of that which is in me but is not my ego.

[1] Among us Nesmelov, who has written a book on St Gregory of Nyssa, very greatly insists upon this.

The soul is a creative process; it is activity.[1] The human spirit must always transcend itself and rise to that which is higher than man; it is only then that man does not lose himself and disappear, but realizes himself. Man disappears in self-affirmation and self-complacency, and hence it is that sacrifice is the path to the realization of personality. Man does not happen as an absolutely lonely being. There is in him the voice of the *daimon*. The Greeks said that the *daimones* are the bestowers of happiness. 'Eudaimon' is he who has received a good *daimon* as his portion. The complexity of man's composition is made greater by this. Jung maintains that *persona* is the mask of a collective reality.[2] But this must on no account be extended to the metaphysical core of personality. Several egos exist but there is the profound ego. Man is confronted by many worlds which correspond to various forms of activity:—the world of prosaic everyday life, the world of religion, the world of science, the world of art, the world of politics, the world of economics, and the rest. And these various worlds stamp their impress upon the formation of personality, upon the way the world is represented; our perception of the world is always an act of choice, an act of limitation, there is much that escapes from our field of consciousness. Every act of ours, such as, for example, the reading of a book, is like that. Amiel truly says that each person understands only what he finds in himself.

Man is both very limited and infinite. He has but little capaciousness and at the same time can find room for the universe. Potentially he includes everything and he actualizes but little. He is a living contradiction, a mingling of the finite and the infinite. In the same way it may be said that man combines both sublimity and baseness. Pascal expressed this better than anyone. The separation of the emotions, the will, or the intellectually apprehensive

[1] Wundt says this and thus reveals himself as an actualist in his conception of the spiritual life.

[2] See Jung, *Le Moi et l'Inconscient.*

processes, exists only in abstract thought, in concrete actuality everything presupposes the whole psychical life. The synthetizing creative act creates the image of man and without it there would be merely a collection and medley of bits and pieces. The enfeeblement of spirituality in man, the loss of the centre, even leads to disintegration into bits and pieces. This is a process of dissolution and dissociation of personality. But the emotional life is the basic fact and the background of human life. Without emotionality, even apprehension is impossible.[1] Carus, an anthropologist and psychologist of the romantic era, thought that the conscious was individual, whereas the unconscious was supra-individual.[2] This is true only in the sense that in the depth of the unconscious man goes out beyond the frontiers of consciousness and enters into union with cosmic elements. But the core of individuality lies deeper than consciousness. The bitter truth must be recognized that it is a natural thing for people to hate and kill one another, but a supra-natural, and a spiritual thing for them to love one another, and help one another. For this reason what should be affirmed is not natural right, natural ethics and natural reason, but spiritual right, spiritual ethics, and spiritual reason. The mistake has been made of relating the integrality and freedom of man to the primitive and the natural, to sources in the phenomenal world, whereas it can only be related to spirit, to the noumenal world. Everything is determined by an act of spirit which rises above the natural cycle. Ravison contrasts *passion* (where the cause lies outside the being who experiences it) and *action* (where the cause is in the being himself).[3] But *action* has the primacy over *passion*, for that which comes from without is a projection and an ejection into the external of that which was within the being himself.

The painful and dramatic nature of human existence depends to

[1] Max Scheler particularly insists upon the importance of emotional intuition, but intuition cannot be emotional in its pure aspect.

[2] See Chr. Bernouilli, *Die Psychologie von Karl Gustav Carus.*

[3] See Ravison, *De L'Habitude.*

a notable degree upon the seclusion of human beings from one another and the weakness of that synthetizing spirituality which leads to inner unity and the union of man with man. Erotic union in actual fact leaves a dreadful dissociation and even hostility. Real union among human beings is evidence of the divine-human link. People can be united only in God-manhood, not in the human; a unity of the human does exist but it is a spiritual unity, a unity of destiny. When men attempt to solve the problem of the perfect human life while they are absorbed in the path which leads to individual moral and religious perfection, they see that the path of social change and perfection is also a necessity. When this same problem is decided by those who are absorbed in the path of social change and perfection, then in turn the necessity makes itself felt of a process for achieving the interior perfection of human beings.

There is a true and a false criticism of humanism (humanitarianism). Its fundamental falsity lies in the idea of the self-sufficiency of man, of the self-deification of man, that is to say in the denial of God-manhood. The aspiration of man and his attainment of the heights presuppose the existence of something higher than man. And when man is left with himself, shut up in his humanity, he makes himself idols without which he cannot rise. Upon this the true criticism of humanism is founded. The false criticism on the other hand denies the positive significance of humanistic experience and leads to the denial of the humanity of man. It may lead to the brutalizing of him when an unhuman god is worshipped. But an inhuman god is in no degree better and is indeed even worse than a godless man. In the history of Christianity an inhuman god has very frequently been affirmed and this has led to the appearance of the godless man. But it must always be remembered that the denial of God and God-manhood at the surface of the mind does not mean the absence of actual God-manhood in men. The highest humanity is embedded in Christianity for it relies upon God-manhood and Christian personalism, upon the recognition of all human personality as the highest value. But in the history of the Christian world three stages may be recognized: inhumanity within Christianity; humanity outside Christianity; and a new Christian humanity. The humanity which lies outside Christianity may easily mean not an attitude to the concrete human being but an attitude to men and mankind in the abstract. This is always liable to end in the fashioning of idols, out of society, out of mankind, out of the idea of justice and so on and so on. But the concrete living creature, this man here before me, is higher in value than the abstract idea of good, of the general well-being, of infinite progress and the like; and this is the Christian attitude to man.[1] There is a real paradox in the fact that this is also the highest idea of humanity and personalism.

It is only Christianity which requires a human attitude to one's enemy, which demands love for one's enemies. But Christians have continued to practise inhumanity in war, in revolutions and in counter-revolutions, in the punishment of those whom they consider criminals, and in conflict with those who hold a different faith or are of a different way of thinking. In the life of societies the human has depended upon the level of moral development in the societies. Absolute Christian truth has been adjusted to the sphere of the relative and has readily become distorted. On the other hand moralistic normativism and legalism may easily become inhuman. In Kant who rendered great services in the sphere of moral philosolhy it is not so much the concrete man who is of unconditional value as the ethical and rational nature of man.[2] Moralistic formalism always has bad effects and distorts the immediate vital relation of man to man. The same thing has to be said also of Tolstoy's moralism. The sociological view of the

[1] See my book, *The Destiny of Man.*

[2] See an interesting criticism of Kantian ethical formalism in Max Scheler, *Der Formalismus in der Ethik und die materiale Wertethik.*

world, which is replacing theology by sociology, may inscribe humanity on its banners but one cannot find in it any relation to the concrete man. The primacy of society over man, over human personality, is maintained.

The existential dialectic which arises from the doctrine of J. J. Rousseau that the nature of man was originally good but that it has been distorted by societies and civilization, is very interesting. It must be said in the first place that in consequence of the weakness of Rousseau's general philosophical position his opponents have been given an easy opening for criticizing him. But this criticism has always admitted an error. In Rousseau the good nature of man is his nature before the Fall; it is a memory of paradise. The state of civilized society is a fallen one. St Thomas Aquinas also considered that the nature of man is good. Hence the enormous rôle he assigns to natural reason, natural morals and natural law. Evil does not arise from nature but from will. Rousseau starts from a revolt against the structure of society as the source of all evils, as that which oppresses man. But he ends in the conclusion of a Social Contract which is concerned with a new structure of society. But this new state and society will oppress man anew in its turn. The inalienable right and freedom of man and above all freedom of conscience are denied. Rousseau proposes to expel Christians from the new society. This bore its fruit in Jacobinism, which is totalitarian in character. Tolstoy was more consistent and thorough-going. He has no desire to conclude any sort of social contract; he proposes point blank to remain in divine nature. But on the other hand the doctrine of the sinfulness of human nature has readily lent itself to interpretation in a way that is degrading to man and inhuman. In classical Calvinism and in the Barthianism of to-day man is debased, they look upon him as a mere nothing. But where the audacity of man is exalted, as in Kant, there also man is denied and destroyed; he disappears in the superman. I have already spoken about the dialectic of the human and the divine in Nietzsche. Marx also in the same way starts with the defence of man, with humanism, and ends with the disappearance of man in society, in the social collective. Along different lines both Nietzsche and Marx arrive at a denial of humanity, at a breach with both the ethics of the Gospel and with humanitarian ethics; but Marx denies humanity to a much smaller extent and opens up the possibility of a neo-humanism, The whole creative work of Dostoyevsky was full of the emotional dialectic of the relation between the divine-human and the human-divine. Humanity cannot be taken separately in disruption from the supra-human and the divine, and the human which is self-asserting easily passes into inhumanity.

For the construction of a religious anthropology it is of great importance to understand the part which sex plays in human life. The curse of sex hangs over man. Man is not a whole creature; a whole creature would be androgynous; man is a being divided into halves, that is to say he is a sexual creature. He yearns and struggles for completion, for the attainment of the wholeness which he never does attain or attains only for a moment. There is no sphere of life in which so much that is ugly and banal has accumulated as it has around sex. Man hides his sex as a thing to be ashamed of. Sex is experienced not only as the source of life and of what may be an uplifting vital impulse, but also as the degradation and slavery of man. The world is passing through a crisis of birth, and it is very sick. This crisis is connected with a sharpening of the individual personal consciousness. Man can no longer live the old life in this respect and this is due to the part played by the machine. The entry of the machine into human life is producing a terrible revolution.[1] The principle of organism is being replaced by that of organization, and the cosmic by the social.

One must not confuse the sexual and the erotic; they are two

[1] See my pamphlet, *Man and the Machine*.

principles which are intertwined, but they are distinct. The union of the sexes is a biological, animal principle; the family is a social principle, linked with the begetting of children; love is a metaphysical, personal principle. As regards the first, there should be established a delimiting *askesis*, and even an *askesis* which surmounts it completely; and for the second, a free comradeship and brotherhood. For the third no standards at all are possible, because love is freely mystical and unrepeatably individual in character; it is not subject to the laws of the world; and it sometimes demands free sacrifice. Racism is anti-human and anti-Christian, it is based entirely upon the principle of biological heredity which is open to grave doubt from the biological point of view.[1] It is extreme anti-personalism and looks upon man as a breed of animals. It is a mistake to think that through racial selection, which is very reminiscent of cattle-breeding, an aristocratic race will be created. Such a selection, which is biological and social is a plebeian principle, for the desire to manoeuvre oneself into the first rank is a plebeian desire. The aristocratic spirit can be nothing but original and innate. Aristocracy is spirit; matter is always plebeian. Real aristocracy is the aristocracy which stoops, an aristocracy of sacrifice. There must be a feeling of guilt and of pity at the base of it. Two ideas wrestle with each other in the world—(1) the selection of the strong, of the best, of the thorough-bred, of the aristocrats of blood and race; the lordship of some human beings over others, and (2) the brotherhood of man, the dignity and value of every human personality, the recognition of the spiritual basis of personality. For those who cherish the first idea man is merely nature; for the second idea man is spirit. The truly human is linked with the second idea; the first idea is unhuman.

But there is a dialectic of the first and the last. The last become first and everything is left in a hopeless circle from which there is no way out. And to this day racial ethics determine moral values;

[1] See Jean Rostand, *Hérédité et racisme.*

to this day illusory feelings maintain their hold upon men. The ethics of the tribe are still strong. With this is associated a false conception of honour, of family, tribal and national honour, the honour of class and of the army, which takes the place of the true idea of the dignity and worth of personality. To this day Christains have but a poor understanding of the fact that what degrades a man is what issues from him and not what enters into him. Idealized instincts of revenge even to this day take possession of Christians. The ethics of the truly human come into collision with a moral contradiction and paradox. When a man strives after purity and perfection, when he is wounded by the evil of the world and professes a moral maximalism, not only does this not guarantee his true humanity but it may even lead to inhumanity. The examples of the Montanists, Manichaeans, Catharists, Puritans, Jansenists, Jacobins, Tolstoyans, fanatical believers in communism and many others, show how complex and difficult is the attainment of real humanity. The moral paradox is that publicans and sinners may enter first into the Kingdom of Heaven. The distinguishing characteristic of Christianity is its love for sinners. It may be the case that no mercy is to be found among the pure, those who have kept their garments white. It is a mistake and even hypocritical to separate oneself from the world, as one who is pure. It is from this that the monastic disdain of the world and men comes, and a puritanical appraisement of people. Such is the existential dialectic of striving after one's own purity.

The most difficult thing of all is to defend and maintain the human in the life of societies. Yet, as a matter of fact, humanity is the basis of the society which men desire and which ought to be. We ought to strive after a new society, one which recognizes the highest value in man, not in the State or in society or in the nation. The human masses have been governed and they continue to be governed by scrambling bread and providing circuses; they are governed through the agency of myths, of sumptuous religious

:remonies and festivals, and through hypnosis and propaganda, ıd most of all by bloody violence. This is manlike, all too man-ke, but it is not human. In politics an enormous rôle is played by .lsehood and there is but little room for truth. States have been uilt upon lies and upon lies they have been wrecked. It is indeed ften said that without falsehood everything in this world would erish and complete anarchy would ensue. Machiavellianism is ot some special sort of line in the politics of the Renaissance; it on the contrary the essence of politics, which are regarded as ıtonomous and free from moral restrictions. Machiavellianism is ractised by conservatives and revolutionaries alike, and hitherto ıere has been no revolution which has been directed against the nrestricted power of politics, in the name of man and his true umanity. Man ought not to endure the outrage of human dig-ity; he ought not to endure violence and slavery; it is in this that ıe moral justification of revolution lies. But not all the means hich revolution may employ can be justified. Revolution may self perpetrate outrage upon human dignity; it may ravish and nslave. Clothes change but man remains what he was of old, and ıe truly human does not triumph. That demands a deeper and a piritual revolution. Too often men have interpreted the bearing f one's cross as meaning submissiveness to evil, and meek resigna-ion in the face of evil. This has been one of the causes of the revolt gainst Christianity. But the uncontaminated meaning of Chris-ian humility is something entirely different. It means the inward piritual act of overcoming ego-centricity, not a servile submis-iveness. People constantly perform myth-creating actions in order o please their ego-centricity. They create myths about themselves, bout their ancestors, about their native land, about their class and ank, about their party and their affairs, in order to improve their osition. There are almost no people at all who are free from this reating of myths. Here indeed inward acts of humility are needed, ut it is precisely here that they are least of all demanded.

The will to power both in oneself and in others must be subdued.[1] The deification of men of power, kings, captains, leaders, is an anti-Christian, anti-human lie and enslaves man. It is the worship of power and not of truth. The cultus of the saints has a different meaning and has a positive spiritual significance. But that also may assume false and idolatrous forms. In contrast to what is almost a deification of men of authority and power, reverence for the really great, for men of genius, for creative men, prophets, apostles, reformers, philosophers, the learned, inventors, poets, artists, musicians, and the rest, expresses a noble veneration for that spiritual and creative greatness which is constantly persecuted in the world.[2] We must not forget the fate of the greatest philosopher of India and its religious regenerator, Shankara, who was excommunicated as a heretic, and whose mother they even refused to bury. People who are out of the ordinary, men of genius, on the one hand are lonely and misunderstood; they do not submit themselves to the influence of their environment and time, but on the other hand they are not shut up in themselves; they express the spirit of universal movement while living before their time. But the formation of an exclusive and proud élite is absolutely wrong. The most remarkable and creative people emerge not in groups but individually; they are, however, individually linked with the deep life of the people. The most creative individualities break out through the enslaving circle of objectivization towards real existence. The final limit of objectivization would be the turning of man into an ant and society into an ant-heap. Objectivization rests upon law and the norm; it is unaware of the mystery of the individual. If law alone existed the life of man would be intolerable. There must also exist a sphere which lies outside law, a sphere which is unrepeatably individual.

[1] See my book, *Slavery and Freedom*.

[2] Carlyle in his *Heroes and Heroworship* confuses these two kinds of reverence.

But the proneness of man to objectivization is with difficulty overcome; upon it all kingdoms in the world have calmly rested, and all pagan religions connected with the tribe and the City-state. The truly human makes a stand against objectivization; for it is not the socialization but the spiritualization of human life. The social problem is the problem of the human. Not only does the world environment and the social environment influence man but he also projects his own interior experiences out into them. Expressiveness issues out of the depth and it is that which determines community and the communion of human beings. Man ought above all things to be free and this is to say something much more profound than that man has a right to freedom. It is impossible to create a free society out of servile souls. Society in itself cannot make a man free. It is man that must make society free because he himself is a free spiritual being. The pendulum swings between the old régime, a totalitarianism which imposes obligatory beliefs (the age of Augustus and the age of Louis XIV) which is characterized by the absence of freedom, and the subjection of personality to society and the State, and on the other hand the facility of superficial democracies, the unbelief and scepticism of liberal régimes. The truth is in a third, in a creative labouring society. Man is a creative being, not only in a cosmic but also in a theogonic sense. But contradiction and dividedness run through the whole of life. Kaiserling truly says that creativeness is also destruction and the acceptance of life is also the acceptance of death. As compared with the ancient world Christianity has greatly strengthened, developed and refined the inner life of man, but at the same time it has been the source of great disquietude about the destiny of man. This was shown completely not in the Middle Ages but in modern times. In earlier centuries feeling was concealed behind ceremonies, symbols, and external ornamentation; it became more sincere in the nineteenth and twentieth centuries. The sensitiveness of Rousseau, the melancholy of

Chateaubriand, Senancourt and Amiel was a new manifestation in the story of the European soul and a still newer phenomenon was the tragic outlook of Kierkegaard, Dostoyevsky and Nietzsche.

The human is associated with love and pity. A human person is one who loves and pities. There is in this world no higher principle than pity. But as with every principle in this world, pity cannot be an exclusive principle; it must be combined with the feeling of freedom and dignity. Into eros-love pity too must enter; otherwise it becomes demonic and destructive. Men dispute about the relation between eros-love and agape-love; it is a question which has been raised in a particularly clear-cut form in Nygren's book.[1] Eros is desire, yearning, it is a sense of lack. In this sense the gods cannot love, they lack nothing. Eros is egoistic. Eros-love loves the divine in man, not the man himself. Such was Platonism. Nygren is inclined to assign negative properties to eros. But eros-love cannot but lead on to real love, for in love there is a capacity for rapture, and an upward rush towards the divine heights. The limits of the platonic eros lie in the fact that in itself it is love not so much for man as for the divine; it is love for God in man and not for man himself. In this respect there is a lack of the really human in eros. To Nygren agape is creative love and at the same time love which has no motive. The love of God Himself is of that kind; in Him there cannot be eros-love. But in spite of what Nygren says, even in God too there can be yearning for the beloved, and for responsive love. It is unexplained how agape-love can be in man; it becomes, so to speak, a privilege of God.

In actual fact there must be a union of eros-love and agape-love. Man's love is a more complex thing than the scheme of these two types of love. Love which is pity, sympathy, *caritas*, is covered neither by eros nor by agape, for it is love for the created thing

[1] See Nygren, *Eros et Agape*.

in its Godforsakenness. The experience of love is the most stupendous experience man has and in it there takes place a real act of transcendence over the immanent cycle of this world. Love is connected with personality, it is a relation between one personality and another.[1] Love is really human when it is love not only for God in man, for what is perfect and beautiful in him, but also for man in God, for the unrepeatable individual, one who is dear to me independently of any perfection he may or may not have. Love ought to be inspired and permeated by the spiritual, but it cannot be exclusively spiritual; it is spiritually-psychical and even spiritually-corporeal. It has an immediate relation to the unrepeatably individual. Love is divine-human, and it is only so that it can be human. Love conquers death; in it the vistas of immortality are opened up. In the experience of love the Kingdom of God begins to reveal itself. Be human, be pitiful, be loving and then the pathway to immortality will open out. The fundamental difference among people is the difference between those who love and pity and those who do not love and do not pity; and this is the difference between 'good' and 'bad' people. No less important is the difference between those who are real true human beings and those who are not, between truthful people and untruthful.

Not only does the humanization of man himself take place, that is to say the disclosure of his human-ness, but there is also the humanization of his natural and social environment. The humanization of man's idea of God also occurs, and that simply means a liberation from false anthropomorphism. Paradoxically it has to be said that the impress of the human is not the impress of anthropomorphism but the impress of theomorphism. For human-ness is divine; it is not man that is divine, but human-ness. Human-ness is an integral attitude to man and to life, not only to the world of mankind but also to the world of animals. Human-ness is the

[1] On the types of love see P. Florensky, *The Pillar and Ground of the Truth*, and Max Scheler, *Nature et formes de la sympathie*.

revelation of the fullness of human nature, that is to say the disclosure of the creative nature of man. This creative nature of man ought to show itself also in a human attitude of man to man.

It is sometimes said that a new man ought to make his appearance; it is Christian terminology. Christianity was the proclamation of the appearance of the new Adam, of victory over the old Adam. Man ought eternally to be becoming new, that is he ought to be giving effect to the fullness of his humanity. There does not exist an absolutely unchanging human nature, such as was imagined by Aristotle, St Thomas Aquinas and Kant (although in different ways), such as theology in its prevailing forms imagines, and in company with it many a philosopher of the rationalistic type. Man changes, he progresses and regresses; his consciousness expands and deepens, but it also contracts and is thrown on to the surface. Even more profound changes of human consciousness are possible, as a result of which the world will take on a different appearance. Nothing but a dynamic conception of man is true. But with all that God's design for man remains the same. It is a project for eternal human-ness, for complete human-ness. Man will never be replaced by the superman or by the spirit of other hierarchies, as theosophists and occultists think. Man will inherit eternity in his human-ness; he is called to life in God; he moves from eternity through time towards eternity. The new man may represent creative enrichment in the realization of the fullness of his humanity. But he may represent a treachery to the idea of man, he may be a perversion of it; he may be a manifestation, not of God-manhood but of beast-manhood, that is to say he may deny his human-ness.

The new man may also find himself standing face to face with the abyss of non-being, and confronted by the attraction of non-being.[1]

[1] In this respect the new movement in France is characteristic. See Sartre, *L'Etre et le Néant*; Bataille, *L'Expérience intérieure*; A. Camus, *Le Mythe de Sisyphe*. This movement is complex. In the last resort Sartre draws a conclusion in the spirit of neo-humanism, and so does Camus.

Present-day man, oppressed by fallen and disintegrating being, is being captivated by non-being. Face to face with the very brink of non-being he wants to experience the final ecstasy, whether the ecstasy of heroism for the sake of nothingness, or the ecstasy of creativeness which arises out of his own nothingness. Nietzsche was already moving towards the abyss. In the rush of his creative genius he arrived not at the new man but at the destruction of man, at the replacement of him by something entirely different, by a non-human creature in which the human disappears. Revolutionary social movements may also arrive at the betrayal of the human. It is in the God-man, in the Son of God and the Son of Man, that the new man takes his beginning, the man of a new and eternal humanity.

In the language of traditional terminology God-manhood corresponds to the union of grace and freedom. From this there also arises a new ethic, one which stands in opposition to the old racial ethic, which is based upon an idealization of the ancient instincts of revenge, envy, possession, of servile submissiveness before power and authority, upon a false understanding of class honour, upon false feelings towards the collective reality, upon the confusion of belief with fanaticism and exclusiveness. The ethics of the human, the ethics of personalism, must be constructed upon an attitude which regards man, personality, as the highest value, it must be founded upon the unrepeatably individual and not on the impersonal common.[1] The new ethic of the new man will above all be an ethic of creativeness, not of law; but of the creativeness of man and of the human, not the creativeness of a being which is no longer man. The human is connected with spirituality.

[1] My book, *The Destiny of Man*, was an attempt to construct such an ethic.

CHAPTER IX

Spirituality

The acquisition of spirituality is the chief problem of human life, but spirituality must be taken in a wider sense than that in which it is commonly understood. Spirituality is a necessity even in the struggle which man carries on in the world. Without spirituality it is impossible to make sacrifices or to achieve heroic feats. Joy in the light of the sun is spiritual joy; the sun is spiritual. The form of the human body and the countenance of man are spiritual. Great spirituality may be possessed even by a man, who, so far as the surface of his thought is concerned, and in many cases through a misunderstanding, considers himself a materialist. Chernishevsky may be taken as a case in point. If a philosophy of spirituality can be constructed it will in no case be the abstract subject which has borne that name in the schools, and which was a form of naturalistic metaphysics. Spirit is not a substance.[1] Spirit is not only a different reality from that of the natural world, it is indeed reality in another sense altogether. Spirit is freedom and free energy, which breaks through into the natural and historical world. It is essential to affirm a relative truth in dualism, without which the independence of spiritual life is not to be understood. But the dualism is not of spirit and matter or of spirit and body; it is above all the dualism of freedom and necessity. Spirit is freedom, not nature. Spirit is not a constituent part of human nature; it is, rather, the highest qualitative value. The spiritual quality and spiritual value of man are determined not by nature, of any sort, but by the union of freedom and grace.

Spirit is revolutionary in relation to the natural and historical

[1] See my book, *Spirit and Reality*.

orld; it is a break-through from the other world into this world, nd it overthrows the coercive order of this world. Emancipation om slavery, that is the fundamental fact of world life. But the tal mistake of liberators has been to suppose that the liberation omes from the material, from nature. Freedom comes from irit. A still more fatal mistake, and this on the part of the de- nders of spirit, has been to think that spirit does not liberate, ut that it connects with, and subordinates to, authority. Both the ne group and the other have thought mistakenly about spirit, and ave prepared the way for a veritable *progrom* upon spirituality. pirit is not only freedom, it is also meaning. The meaning of the orld is spiritual. When it is said that life and the world have no eaning, the existence of a meaning at a higher level than life and e world is thereby acknowledged, that is to say judgment is assed upon the meaninglessness of world life from the point of iew of spirit. Jaspers says truly that spirit occupies a paradoxical osition between opposites. Spirit and spirituality remake, trans- orm, and illuminate the natural historical world; they bring reedom and meaning into it.

Objectivization of spirit takes place, and it is regarded as incar- ation and realization. But objectivized spirit is spirit alienated rom itself, spirit which loses its fire, its creative youth and strength; t is spirit accommodated to the everyday world, to the average evel.[1] We cannot speak of objective spirit, as Hegel spoke. The ruth is that only subjective spirit exists, or spirit which lies beyond oth the subjective and the objective. Objective spirituality is a neaningless expression. Spirituality is always subjective; it lies utside objectivization. Objectivization is, as it were, the withering nd mortification of spirit. Spirituality is outside the phenomenal bjectivized world, it does not develop out of it, it simply breaks hrough into it. We cannot believe in progressive triumph in the evelopment of spirit and spirituality in history, as Hegel believed.

[1] I develop this thought in my forthcoming book, *Creativeness and Objectivity*.

The loftiest expressions of spirituality in the world do not convey the impression of being the result of a gradual development of spirit in history.

The attainment of spirituality is liberation from the power of the world and social environment. It is, as it were, a break-through of the noumenal into the phenomenal. The growth of spirituality in man does not belong to the rhythmic regularity of an evolutionary process. Where freedom operates there is no process controlled by necessity; where creativeness acts there is no evolution in the naturalistic sense of the word. Spirituality is a task, a problem set before man in relation to life. There is a paradox in the fact that the growth of spirituality is realized by the very spiritual strength which is in man; this growth cannot be the result of conditions which are not spiritual. The higher is never received from the lower, from that which contained no germs of the higher in it, no potentiality of the higher. Spiritual development is the actualization of the possible. An experience of life which contains nothing spiritual may appear to arouse spiritual strength in a man; for example, suffering from sickness or from want or from injustice or treachery, but in reality the arousing of spiritual strength presupposes that it has always been there, latent, in a hidden unawakened state. Freedom, which is in opposition to nature, is always spirit. The mistake of the naturalistic evolutionary theory consists in the supposition that the lower in itself gives rise to the higher, that the material has it in its power to create the spiritual. Spiritual power in man is in its origin not human only, but divine-human. Spirituality is a divine-human condition. Man in his spiritual depths comes into touch with the divine, and from the divine source he receives support.

There is no necessary evolution in the spiritual history of the world, such as Hegel supposed, and many others after him. What we see in the history of the world is objectivization of spirit. But the objectivization of spirit is the diminution of it. Objectivization is the opposite of transcendence, that is to say, of movement towards God. But it would be a mistake to regard the process of objectivization of spirituality, which finds its expression in the evolution of civilization, merely negatively. In the condition of this phenomenal world, it has a positive significance also. It contributes to the subjugation of the wild, barbarous, animal nature of man, and the consciousness of man really begins to grow. But this is an elementary process and the heights of spirituality are not attained by it. And, moreover, we can never exactly define where true spirituality reveals itself, it may not be at all at the high points of civilization that it is revealed. It is very important to understand further that spirituality is by no means opposed to the soul and the body; it takes control of them and transfigures them. Spirit is above all a liberating and transforming power. A man of strongly expressed spirituality is by no means necessarily a man who has withdrawn from the world and historical life. He is a man who dwells in the life of the world and history and is active in it, but he is free from its power and is engaged in transforming it.

The spirituality which turns its back upon the pluralist world, as, for example, a certain form of spirituality in India, in Plotinus, and in monastic asceticism, cannot be regarded as Christian; it contradicts the divine-human character of Christianity and the command of Christ about love for one's neighbour. Christian spirituality is not only an ascent; it is also a descent, and it is only such spirituality that is truly human. A form of spirituality which is inhuman and hostile to man is also a possibility; and such a declension has frequently taken place. But man ought to accept responsibility not only for his own destiny and for the destiny of those who are near to him, but also for the destiny of his people, of mankind and of the world. He must not separate himself from his people and the world and proudly dwell alone on the spiritual heights. The danger of pride lies in wait upon the spiritual path, and much warning has been given of that fact. This danger is always a result of that same disruption of the divine-human link. An example of such pride is provided by the Brahmins who claim to be supermen. It belongs also to certain forms of occultism. The needful thing is to strive after the human spirituality which is also divine-human spirituality.

Not only is there Christian spirituality and non-Christian spirituality, but within Christianity itself there are various types of it, for example Orthodox spirituality and Catholic spirituality.[1] But spirituality has its universal and eternal foundations. Indian spirituality is very profound. The mystics of all times and all peoples hail one another. Prayer has an eternal significance. Man is a praying creature and even those who do not consider themselves believers feel the need of prayer. In what does the essence of prayer consist?[2] Prayer is evoked by the need to feel oneself not entirely dependent upon the necessity which reigns in the world, and upon the power of fate which belongs to this world. Prayer is conversation with the Existent One who is exalted above the world cycle, above that falsity and wrongness in which the world is submerged. Christian spirituality is distinguished from non-Christian spirituality by the fact that personality, freedom and love are always affirmed in it. Spirituality in which the unrepeatable person disappears, and in which there is no freedom of man or love for man, must be regarded as unchristian. The spirituality which might be called monistic, that is to say, which denies the independence of human nature, is not Christian.

The spirituality of India, sublime as it is in itself, is cold in comparison with Christian spirituality, just because of its pantheistic character, which metaphysically denies the principle of personality. Aurobindo, in his commentaries upon the *Bhagavad-gita*, says that the wise man is benevolent to all alike; that he is characterized by indifference to everything, by absence of desire, and by

[1] See my book, *Spirit and Reality*. [2] See Heiler, *Das Gebet*.

enial of the distinction between the happy and the unhappy.[1] imilar ideas have arisen in Christian spirituality also, especially ı Syrian ascetic spirituality and in the *Dobrotolyubie*. The same everance from the multiple world is to be found in the mysticism f Plotinus and of neoplatonism. But true Christian spirituality is hristological, that is to say it is divine-human. In it man cannot isappear in an apathetic identification and unity. Divine-human pirituality may begin with the consciousness of the sinfulness and nworthiness of man, submerged as he is in the elements of the vorld, but it must assert the dignity of man as a being in the likeess of God and foreordained to eternity. The bitter feeling which rises from the knowledge of human baseness ought not to coneal the high destiny to which man is foreordained.

Christian spirituality is not coldly dispassionate; it is a burning lame; in it a sense of emancipation and of severance from the lements of the world is combined with taking a share in the lestiny of the world, of mankind and of all suffering creation. pirituality ought to transform, not to crush the passionate nature f man. Christianity liberates man from the elemental spirits of ature and in so doing affirms the independence and freedom of nan and of spirit. But this by no means indicates indifference to he world and to man. In the very foundations of Christianity there ies the command to love God and to love one's neighbour, and herein lies its divine-human, its truly human character. This is the ntithesis of a sundered and aloof indifference to the multiple vorld. Love for one's neighbour is love for the multiple world. To turn towards the One does not mean to turn away from the nany, and from what is individual in the world.

But spirituality, like everything else in this world, is objecivized. It takes on a formal and legal character; it cools down; it is ccommodated to prosaic social normality and is adapted to the verage man. The unspiritual character of the so-called spiritual

[1] See the book already cited, *Le Bhagavad-gita, interprété par Shri Aurobindo*.

life in the official Churches and Confessions is appalling. A conventional, rhetorical, token spirituality is elaborated and it has aroused disgust for Christianity. More profound significance attaches to the fact that spirituality was originally connected with myth. Every significant myth is connected with reality, but this connection may be loosened, and an eager desire for right and truthfulness in the spiritual life may give rise to a need to liberate spirituality from the myth. This will mean a transition from symbolism to realism, to mystical realism.

The depth of the ego in man is connected with spirituality; spirit is the principle which synthetizes, and maintains the unity of personality. Man must all the while perform a creative act in relation to himself. In this creative act the self-realization of personality comes to pass. It is a constant struggle against the multiplicity of false egos in man. Chaos stirs within man; he is connected with the chaos which is hidden behind the cosmos. Out of this chaos are born illusory, false egos. Every passion by which a man is possessed can create an ego which is not the real ego, which is *Es*. In the struggle for personality, for the real, the deep ego, there takes place a process of dissolution—this is a danger which eternally lies in wait—and a process of synthesis, of integration. Man is in greater need of psycho-synthesis than of psycho-analysis, which in itself may lead to the disintegration and collapse of personality.

Spirituality, issuing out of the depth, is also the power which shapes and maintains personality in man. Blood, heredity, race, have merely a phenomenal significance as also, in general, the biological individual. Spirit, freedom, personality, have a noumenal significance. Sociologists maintain that human personality is formed by society, by social relations, that organized society is the source of the highest morality. But the action of society upon man, coming upon him from without, demands adaptation to every-day social normality, to the requirements of the State and to the code of behaviour established by the nation. This throws man into the atmosphere of the useful lie which guards and guarantees. A feeling for truth and right leads man to a conflict with society. That which is spiritually most significant in man certainly does not come from social influences, not from his social environment; it comes from within, not from without.

The primacy of society, the dominance of society over man, leads to the turning of religion into a weapon of the tribe and the State, and to the denial of freedom of the spirit. Roman religion was based upon a strong sense of social life, but from the spiritual point of view it was religion of a very low type. Historical Christianity has been distorted by social influences and adjustments. The social regimentation of man has led to indifference to truth and right. Every system of social monism is hostile to freedom of the spirit. The conflict between spirit and organized society with its legalism is an eternal conflict. But it would be a mistake to interpret this as individualism and a lack of any sense of society. On the contrary, it must be insisted upon that there is an inward sociality, that man is a social being and that he can realize himself completely only in society. But a better, a more just and really human society can be created only from the spiritual sociality of man, from an existential source and not from objectivization.

Society which is deified is from the metaphysical point of view, a reactionary principle. A break-through of spirituality into social life is possible, and everything which is best in social life is derived from that source. Spirituality brings liberation with it; it brings a human-ness with it; whereas the domination of objectivized society brings enslavement with it. The absolutely false idea current in the second half of the nineteenth century, that man is the creation of his social environment, must be abandoned. On the contrary the social environment is the creation of man. This does not mean that the social environment does not act upon man; it does so in a high degree. But the servile social environment which enslaves man is the outcome of a servile condition of man it is a creation of servile souls. If there is no God then I am the slave of the world. The existence of God is the guarantee of my independence of the world, of society, of the State.

Dostoyevsky says that man sometimes believes in God through pride. The saying is a paradox; but socially its significance is this that man does not consent to prostrate himself before the world society and people, and that he does worship God as the one source of his independence and freedom from the power of the world There is pride in a good sense in unwillingness to worship anybody or anything except God. Spirituality, which is always connected with God, is the finding of inward strength; it is resistance to the power of the world and society over man. They are mad who think that I am impoverished by the fact that God exists that God is the alienation of my own riches (Feuerbach). No— become immeasurably rich from the fact that God exists. I am very poor if only I myself exist and there is nothing higher than I nothing greater than I. And the whole world is terribly poor tame and dull, if it is sufficient unto itself, if there is no Mystery behind it.

In addition to the kind of spirituality which is dealt with in the books on mysticism which describe the pathway of the soul to God, and the experience of communion with God, there is also another and entirely different type of spirituality, which may be called prophetic. Prophetism is divine inspiration; it is listening to the inward voice of God about the destiny of the world and mankind, and about the future. The man of prophetic inspiration stands alone; he is often stoned by the people whom he serves, but in a spiritual sense he is socially minded; he is concerned with society. The path of human prophetic inspiration is not the way of methodical ascent; it is the way of interior irradiation. Prophetic spirituality is entirely different from the spirituality elaborated in the mystical schools of India and Greece. It is spirituality of the ancient Hebrew, Persian and Christian type. But Christianity combines the two types of spirituality in itself.

Spirituality is connected either with individual eschatology or with universal historical eschatology. Primitive Christianity inherited ancient Hebrew messianism which was concerned with the destiny of history, and Greek mysticism which was concerned with the attainment of individual immortality in the mysteries. For this reason we shall see that in the Christian doctrine of immortality there are two strata (the individual immortality of the soul and the resurrection of the dead in the flesh) which it is not very easy to combine in a unity. But spirituality is always a preparation and a pledge of immortality. The natural structure of man is not in itself immortal, he becomes immortal in virtue of his being possessed by spirit, by the principle which brings the human and the divine into touch with each other. Love is the great spiritual force, and it vanquishes death and wins immortality; it is stronger than death. Love is connected with personality and it demands that personality shall be immortal.

Nygren, in the book to which I have already referred sees the essence of Christianity in agape and connects it with the sense of community, that is to say with the Church. In eros man is lifted up to God; in agape God lowers Himself to man. God loves because He loves, not as a result of any qualities in the object of His love. But that is just what real human love is also. We cannot fit the most mysterious phenomenon of world life, love, into the scheme of 'eros' and 'agape'. In Nygren's view mysticism and gnosis stand in the eros-tradition and for that reason he rejects them. In this way Christianity is much impoverished. In all its forms spirituality is a struggle for eternity. Real humanity requires a struggle for eternity, for death is the most inhuman of principles.

Spirituality in religious phraseology is the revelation of the Holy Spirit in the world and in man. But the Holy Spirit does not yet reveal Himself completely; He is not yet poured out in fullness upon the life of the world. A new spirituality is possible, a divine-human spirituality in which man reveals himself in his creative strength, to a greater extent than he has revealed himself hitherto. Creativeness, freedom, love more than all else will characterize the new spirituality. It must give an answer to the agony of the world, to the unendurable suffering of man. The old spirituality does not now give an answer. But before the outpouring of light a thickening of the darkness is inevitable. Before a new intensity of spirituality a visible weakening of spirituality is possible. Before the new God-manhood comes to pass, outbreaks of inhumanity may take place, which indicate a state of God-forsakenness in man. The existential dialectic of the divine and the human has not yet come to an end and reached its limit, but sometimes it touches upon the limit and the end, and man stands on the brink of the abyss. The expectation of a new spirituality is the expectation of a new revelation of the Holy Spirit in man and through man. It cannot be a merely passive awaiting; it can only be an active condition in man. If man were doomed to await the event from above, in trepidation and passivity, spirituality would not be divine-human, and divine-humanity would not be possible. Paracletism has more than once revealed itself in Christian history, but the time had not yet come, the hour had not yet struck. There are many grounds for thinking that the time and the hour are approaching.

CHAPTER X

Beauty

Beauty is a characteristic of the highest qualitative state of being, of the highest attainment of existence; it is not a separate side of existence. It may be said that beauty is not only an aesthetic category but a metaphysical category also. If anything is perceived and accepted by man integrally, as a whole, that precisely is beauty. We speak of a beautiful soul, a beautiful life, a beautiful action and so on. This is not merely an aesthetic appraisement, it is an integral appraisement. Everything in life which is harmonious is beauty. An element of beauty lies in all congruity. Beauty is the final goal of the life of the world and of man. The good is a means, it is a path, and it has arisen in opposition to evil (the knowledge of good and evil). Beauty lies beyond the knowledge of good and evil. The good indeed lies beyond the distinction between good and evil, when the evil is already forgotten, and then the good is beauty. There can be no moral deformity in beauty, that is a property of evil. The beauty of evil is an illusion and a fraud. The Kingdom of God can be thought of only as the reign of beauty. The transfiguration of the world is a manifestation of beauty. And all beauty in the world is either a memory of paradise or a prophecy of the transfigured world. The experience of every harmonious state is an experience of beauty. Beauty is the final ideal on the horizon of life, out of which all disharmony, all ugliness and all baseness have been expelled.

A clear distinction must be drawn between beauty and mere prettiness. Prettiness is fraudulent beauty. It relates to the phenomenal world only; in beauty, on the other hand, there is a noumenal principle. But beauty has its own dialectic and the man who tells of it best is Dostoyevsky. He thinks that beauty will save the world. But all the same he says, 'Beauty is not only a terrible, but also a mysterious thing. It is here that the devil strives with God, and the field of battle is the hearts of men.' How are we to understand this? We can indeed say of beauty, that it is a break-through in the struggle and an entering into a communion with the divine world. But beauty is created and revealed in a world of darkness, a world in the grip of passionate conflict. And in the souls of men it may be involved in the clash of contradictory principles. The greatest beauty may exist in tragedy. Dostoyevsky was himself a tragic writer. Tragedy is the clash of contradictory principles; it does not depict harmonious life. But Aristotle's doctrine of katharsis speaks of the experience of beauty through tragedy. Tragic beauty is more profound than its other forms, the divine light is in it.

Externally harmonious beauty may be deceptive and false, it may screen ugliness. Beauty may pass over into its opposite, as may every other principle too, when it breaks away from the source of light. It may, therefore, be said with equal truth, that it is harmony and rest from painful struggle, and that it may become a 'field of battle' between God and the devil. The devil seeks to make use of beauty for his own purposes. Beauty is a great joy in our suffering world, both the beauty of nature and the beauty of art. It is beyond dispute that aesthetic judgments do not include that element of suffering which enters into moral judgments. And it may be for that very reason that the devil seeks to make use of beauty for his own ends. Beauty can become diabolic, not because of its own essential nature, not just because it exists; it may be simply made use of in a conflict between forces which are polar opposites.

Fraudulent beauty is possible, as in the case of the fraudulent beauty of some women, or of the fraudulent beauty of some products of art. The demoniac principle lies not in beauty, nor in creativeness, but in the inward condition and trend of man. The demoniac principle in the works of Leonardo is a favourite topic—for instance in his St John the Baptist and his Gioconda. But the demoniac element, which, it may be, existed in Leonardo himself, was burnt up in his creative act, in which transfiguration was achieved and through which eternity was attained. The environment in which demoniac deviations readily make their appearance is aestheticism, which recognizes only aesthetic values, and replaces all others, e.g. values of truth and goodness by them. But great creators have never been aesthetes. Aestheticism is not a creative condition, it is a state of passivity. The aesthete lives by his environment, he moves in a secondary not a primary world. He is never seeking for truth, nor does he love it, for to him it is an unpleasant reminder. The demoniac deviations which spring up on this soil do not go deep. As a matter of fact I am inclined to think that aesthetes are not even lovers of beauty, for it is not in them to feel attraction towards the divine heights. Aestheticism produces its most poisonous fruits in public life, where it distorts all values. This may be seen in Nietzsche and Leontyev. It is intolerable that anyone should adopt an attitude of hostility towards the realization of greater equity in social life on the ground that in the unjust social régime of the past there was more beauty. The historical aestheticism and romanticism of Leontyev is always false and wrong.

The intuitive perception of beauty in nature, of the beauty of man or of a work of art is the creative mastery of chaos, disintegration and ugliness. It is an act which breaks through the ugly husk which enwraps the world. When the question is asked in books on aesthetics whether beauty is objective or subjective, it is an entirely wrong way of putting the matter. When it is said that beauty is subjective and not objective, what is meant is that it is a subjective illusion, merely a subjective condition of man. Nor is it true to say that beauty is objective. But to say that beauty is subjective is also to say that it is real, for reality is to be found in subjectivity—in that existence which is still full of the primordial flame of life; not in objectivized being in which the fire of life has cooled down.

This leads to the complex problem of the relation between creativity and objectivization or alienation.[1] Is the concrete and tangible expression of every creative act objectivization? Is the beauty, which can be brought into being by the creative forces of nature or the creative power of man, unfailingly 'classical', objective beauty? The controversy between classicism and romanticism is connected with this. Classicism demands, as it were, an objective completeness and finish, that is to say it requires perfection in the products of creation. The same may be the case with the phenomena of nature, they may be classically finished. But nature may be romantic too. The novels of Sir Walter Scott are full of that. Classical objectivity is the attainment of perfection in the finite, it is a sort of triumph over the formless infinite. It was not by chance that the Greeks associated perfection with finitude and were afraid of the infinite as chaos. Romanticism, on the other hand, which really comes to light only in the Christian era, is bent upon the infinite; it does not believe in the attainment of perfection in the finite.

The classical is the same expression of eternal principle as the romantic. Human creativeness cannot but strive after perfection of form, just as it cannot find satisfaction in anything finite and confined to this world. The noumenal, from which creativity issues, ought always to pass beyond the limits of the phenomenal, the finite ought to be shattered by its onrush towards the infinite. The relations between form and the infinite content of life are contradictory and paradoxical. Without form there is no beauty, formlessness is unsightly and it may be an ugly thing. The creative force of life ought to receive form. This is to be seen in the pro-

[1] See my book, *Creativity and Objectivization.*

cesses of nature, in the shaping of the cosmos. But form may become hardened and ossified, it may extinguish the creative fire of life, it may cool it down, it may set limits to it. Then the creative fire must be kindled afresh, it must break up the forms which have become stiff and numb and stream out towards the infinite content.[1] The conflict is eternal and it cannot be brought to an end within the limits of this world. Beauty is linked with form, but beauty is linked also with the creative force of life, with aspiration towards infinity.

To use the phraseology of Nietzsche, Apollo and Dionysus must be combined, they are two eternal principles. The eternal principle of form and the eternal principle of infinite power are to be fused together. Vyacheslav Ivanov says that Dionysus is in himself unsightly. But without Dionysus there is no beauty of Apollo either. The same forces operate also in cosmic life. But beauty is never objectivity in itself, which asks for nothing but mere passivity in relation to itself. Beauty even when it is simply contemplated requires the creative activity of the subject. Beauty is not objectivity, it is always transfiguration. And only creative transfiguration is reality. Really great art has never been purely classical or purely romantic, it could not belong to a conflict of tendencies and could never be wholly objectivized, for eternal life remains in it. The form of great art does not become rigid in mere formalism, the infinite content is linked with it, and aspiration towards infinity. It is so in the case of Shakespeare, of Goethe, of Tolstoy, of Dostoyevsky, of Sophocles, Beethoven, Rembrandt, Michael Angelo and others. So also the beauty of a human face must have form, it could not be beautiful without it, but from behind that form aspiration towards the infinite life must shine out, without that the beauty will be a dead thing. And the beauty of nature must be life, not only form. Benedetto Croce is right

[1] In connection with this question there are some interesting thoughts in Simmel, see his *Lebensanschauung*.

when he connects art above all with expression.[1] Not only is there a particular tendency in art to which the name expressionism is given, but in fact all art and all beauty is expressionism. Beauty is the expression of the infinite life in finite form.

There has been a symbolist movement in art, but it belongs already to the past. There exists, however, an eternal symbolism of art. The truly realistic thing would be, if through art the transfiguration of human life and the life of the world were brought about. But what is provided in art is merely tokens which anticipate real transfiguration. The meaning of art lies in the fact that it anticipates the transfiguration of the world. Art is full of symbols of the other world. Every attainment of beauty is a start upon the transfiguration of the world. The transfiguration is not attained within the confines of art. But art can overstep the boundaries which are laid down for it as a separate sphere of culture. Thus at its highest attainment Russian literature of the nineteenth century was bent upon getting beyond the limits of art, and sought to pass on from the creation of perfect works of art to the creation of the perfect life. Richard Wagner sought to transform the whole of life through a synthesis of music and poetry. The symbolists wanted to overstep the frontiers of art, to go beyond them to something higher than art; but they were not always successful in this. The symbolist feeling for life was liable in such cases to lead to an extreme exaggeration of most insignificant events in their own lives (instances may be found in the cases of Byeli, Blok and others), it might be sham exaltation, it might lose the sense of reality. But there was something of importance there too.

Romanticism, finding no satisfaction in the finiteness of classical art and its confinement within a separate sphere of culture, was often unable to attain what it aspired to reach. But there is a form of art and that the most powerful of all in its action upon the human soul, which in its very nature is romantic rather than

[1] See Benedetto Croce, *Esthétique comme Science de l'expression et générale.*

classical, and that is music. Music is a dynamic art. Its sphere is in movement, in time, but not in space; the finished form of plastic art is not to be found in it, and it in particular gives rise to the stirring of emotion in man and touches his heart profoundly. It is true that we speak of classical music as distinct from romantic, but this is only a conventional expression. The most classical music is that of Bach and it seeks to express the music of the heavenly spheres, not the tragedy of man, as Beethoven's music does. But even Bach's music leads one away from this world into the other and does not leave one in an achieved perfection of form which belongs to this world, which sometimes happens in the case of the plastic arts. It is no mere matter of chance that music is an art which is associated with the Christian era, with the Christian aspiration to pass beyond the boundaries and towards the transcendent.

It was sculpture, on the other hand, which was most characteristic of the Greeks. Painting, however, is a more complex form of art than sculpture; and as regards literature, the most complex, and also the least pure, form of it is the novel, which was characteristic of the nineteenth century soul. Men began to aim not so much at beauty as at truthfulness. This in itself was a gain, but at the same time it led to something which obscured the ideal of beauty. In the end art began to repudiate beauty. Books on aesthetics ceased to connect aesthetic receptivity and aesthetic emotion with beauty. This gives rise to a profound crisis in art. It is to be seen in such movements as futurism, cubism, sur-realism and the rest. Poetry and art are ceasing to be a reminiscence of paradise, they speak rather of hell. Real hell is one of the themes of modern literature (Kafka, for example). In earlier days also art depicted the ugly (Goya, Gogol), but the ugliness was transfigured in the art whereas nowadays they make no effort to achieve such transfiguration. And the attempts to return to classicism are powerless and reactionary. The crisis of art is the crisis of man and it reflects the state of the world. The world is passing into a fluid condition, it is losing its form, there are no longer any solid bodies in it. The solid forms of the cosmos are disappearing in the theories and discoveries of contemporary physics. The solid forms of the human soul are being lost in the discoveries of psycho-analysis and among the philosophers of despair, fear and horror; the solid forms of social life are being lost in the disintegration of the old world, and so on. It is getting more and more difficult for art and literature to attain to solid form.

Weh! Weh!
Du hast sie zerstört
Die Schöne Welt
Mit mächtiger Faust
Sie stürzt, sie zerfällt. (FAUST)

The crisis in art, as also the crisis in all culture, leads on to the subject of eschatology. The immediate sense of the beauty of the cosmos is weakened and beginning to give way, for there is no longer any cosmos. It has been destroyed by the physical sciences and by the power of technical knowledge over the human soul to-day. The machine is being placed between man and nature.[1] The entry upon an epoch which is *par excellence* technical has a metaphysical importance. And in this epoch the human relation to beauty is being revolutionized. Man is losing, as it were, the remnants of his memory of paradise. He is moving forward into a night in which no form is to be seen, but only the shining of stars. Here we come into touch with the end. Among the dissolving forms of the world the worship of the Church possesses the greatest stability, and, as in time past, its beauty powerfully affects the emotional life of man. This is easily understood, for it is there most of all that the divine-human link is preserved. But even in it processes of mortification are possible, unless renovating forms are discovered which express the creative religious process.

[1] See my essay, *Man and the Machine*.

Some thirty years ago I delivered a public lecture on 'The perishing of beauty'. I upheld a pessimistic thesis about the decrease of beauty in the world. Beauty is perishing both in human living which is becoming ever more and more unsightly and lacking in style, and in art which is repudiating beauty more and more. Art seeks to express the bitter truth about man and that truth is unsightly. It is a great service which literature and art render, and they contribute a great deal to the knowledge of life. For the contemplation of plastic beauty men turn to earlier periods. The age of technical skill, the age of masses, the age of overwhelming quantities, the age of acceleration of time, leaves no room for beauty. It looks as though the triumph of greater social justice makes life an unsightly thing; in times of social injustice life was beautiful. It was this more than anything that staggered Constantine Leontyev. Nietzsche was wholly in revolt against the unsightliness of the democratic age. And he turned to the Renaissance, a period which was profoundly immoral, but creative of beauty.

There is a conflict between beauty and goodness and the way out from that conflict is by no means so simple as it appears both to the aesthetes and to the moralists. The union of beauty with truth is the whole transfiguration of life and its illumination, whilst beauty which is divorced from truth and goodness begins to decay and in the end turns into ugliness. There is no progressive growth of beauty in the history of culture, but there is to be traced a refining and sharpening of aesthetic consciousness and aesthetic sensitiveness. Here the rightness of aesthetic pessimism must be recognized. Aestheticism belongs not so much to periods of time marked by the creation of beauty as to periods which were lacking in beauty. The epochs of greatest vigour in the creation of beauty were certainly not those of the greatest quickening of aesthetic consciousness.

It is very natural for people to fall under the influence of aesthetic illusion. We are enraptured by the beauty of historic ruins. But in that past which attracts us there were no ruins, the ruins belong precisely to the present day. We are delighted by the beauty of an ancient church. But the ancient church belongs to our own time. In the past that church was new, it was only just built, it was not an ancient thing. And so with everything else. In the past, that past which attracts the aesthete did not exist, what existed in the past was the present. The fact that the past has grown old is a consolation to us in the ugliness of the present. To remember is a creative force, a transfiguring power, it is by no means a passive condition. We are all the while coming into collision with the paradoxical nature of time. At the present time leaders of new movements of thought and literature in France are arriving at a philosophy of despair, and for them the last word belongs to non-existence. Man is so cunning that he can find consolation even in despair. The greatest influence upon these currents of thought has been that of Nietzsche and Heidegger, and in part also, of Kierkegaard and Shestov: though the influence of these latter took a different direction, as they had religious aspirations. Sartre, Bataille, Camus, are representatives of such movements. In the grip of a sense of the ugliness and loathsomeness of existence, they are trying to find a way of escape in the creative powers of man. But to them man is a mere nothing and a bit of dirt. How can he be a creator, where is he to get the power from? The good in itself is powerless, and does not save. But in itself creativity in art is likewise powerless, and equally does not save. Man stands face to face with the abyss of non-existence, face to face with despair at the outcome of experiencing the breach between the human and the divine, the despair of knowing God-forsakenness. Beauty is not only human, it is divine-human, The journey along the road of the sheer self-assertion and self-sufficiency of man leads to the ruin of beauty. There is here an inescapable dialectic, the dialectic of life itself, not merely of thought. The subject of beauty leads on to the subject of the end and to eschatology. Man treads the way of the Cross to the end.

CHAPTER XI

Immortality

The problem of immortality is fundamental, it is the chief problem of human life, and man only forgets it through superficiality and light-mindedness. Sometimes indeed he likes to persuade himself that he has forgotten it; he does not allow himself to think about the subject which is more important than anything else. The prayer that we may be granted the remembrance of death is a profound prayer, and the seriousness of life itself is conditioned by the remembrance of death, not one's own death only but still more that of other people. All religions, beginning with the rudimentary religious beliefs of savages have taken shape in relation to death. Man is a being who is faced by death throughout his whole life and not only at his last hour. Man wages a double warfare; for life and for immortality. Death is something which is within life and not beyond it; it is the most stupendous of facts, one which borders upon the transcendent.

Great suffering always raises the problem of death and immortality; but every experience which deepens life also always raises the same question. There have been constructed many types of religious and philosophical doctrine of victory over the fear of death and the attainment of real or imaginary immortality. Such are, the spiritualist teaching about the immortality of the soul; the doctrine of reincarnation; the mystical pantheistic doctrine of fusion with the divine; the idealistic doctrine of the immortality of ideas and values; the Christian doctrine of the resurrection of the whole man; the blunting of the edge of the problem of death through fusion with collective life upon earth, and through the possibility of earthly happiness. Spiritualistic teaching about the immortality of the soul promises immortality for part only of man and not for the whole. Still less does the doctrine of reincarnation give immortality to the whole man; it presupposes his dissolution into separate elements, and the precipitation of man into the cosmic cycle. It leaves him in the power of time. Man may pass thus into a non-human kind of existence. The doctrine of fusion with the divine does not mean the immortality of personality but only the immortality of the divine. The idealistic doctrine also does not mean the immortality of the personality but only the immortality of impersonal ideas and values. The avoidance of the subject of immortality by recourse to what I should call social pantheism, concern for the future happiness of mankind, points to the insolubility of the problem and to hostility to the statement of it. It is only the Christian doctrine of the resurrection of the whole man which gives an answer to the question, and with that, as we shall see, many difficulties are associated.

The problem of death and immortality is indissolubly connected with the consciousness of personality and with personal destiny. It is only the death of personality which is tragic. What is tragic is precisely the death of an immortal being. There is nothing in itself tragic about the death of the impersonal; it is only individuality, personality that dies. If the sharp consciousness of personality is lost and its unique and eternal destiny forgotten, one may find consolation in the fact that life in nature and in race eternally renews itself and is immortal. Man as personality fights against death in the name of immortality. The biologists say that death is the price which must be paid for a highly differentiated development. Simmel expresses this in more philosophical terms when he says that life receives form because the living thing dies. But this also means that what dies is that which most demands immortality. Paradoxically this has to be expressed in this way—that which is most subject to death is immortal. So it is from the naturalistic point of view; so it is with the objectivized world.

My favourite cat has died: they will tell me that this death is not tragic because an animal has no personality. This argument is of no importance to me in my experience of deep grief and that for various reasons. An animal in which the great qualities of beauty, intelligence, tenderness, and charm are displayed has a clear individuality, unrepeatable, unique of its kind. This is not personality in the human sense, but all the same it is personality in a different degree. What, however, is most important is that my great love for my cat demands, as all love demands, immortality, eternity for the object of its love. I cannot think of the Kingdom of God without a place in it for my Murya. It is a question of a relationship which is completely personal on my part, and the death of the creature to whom I am not allowed the right to ascribe personality may be a very tragic thing for me. Descartes's theory that an animal has no soul and is a mere mechanism has always stirred me to revolt. The theory seems to me to be stupid and for this reason I have never been able to feel very fond of Descartes. But the denial of the possibility of immortality in the case of animals stirs me to revolt no less. I go further. The death of a tree which I have loved and in which I have found delight may be a tragic thing for me, and my spiritual strength may be exerted for its resurrection.

The belief of the ancients was not in the immortality of man and the human, but in the immortality of the god and the divine.[1] The soul was associated with the breath which issues from the god. The soul has a shadow. There was a very widespread belief that it is necessary to nourish the dead since otherwise hostile action on their part may take place. On the path of the life which lies beyond the tomb they saw hindrances of various kinds, dangerous places that have to be passed through, encounters with wild beasts. In the life after death the struggle was also hard and dangerous. It was only in Egypt that immortality was conditioned by moral

[1] See Addison, *La Vie après la Mort.*

considerations. The Egyptians were the first to recognize the human soul as immortal; but to begin with it was only the king who was regarded as immortal, and then later on, the privileged classes. The soul liberated from the body is immortal because it is divine. The immortality of a grain of wheat was the source of belief in immortality among the Egyptians. Through the rites of Osiris the king became a god. Traces of this belief still remain in the hallowing of kings during the Christian era. The Egyptian king was a collective soul, the soul of the race, a totem; he was identified with Osiris. But in their conception the make-up of man was hightly complex. In each man there is his *Ka*, his twin, his totem, the source of life, the protecting genius; and it is precisely the *Ka* which is immortal. To die means to go to live with one's *Ka*.

The doctrine of reincarnation, which was very widely spread in the ancient world, was connected with the idea of moral compensation, with the evil one had committed in previous reincarnations. In Zoroastrianism resurrection in the flesh already appears. It is highly characteristic that the Greeks connected their hopes of immortality with the soul, while the Hebrews connected it with God. That is why the idea of the immortality of the soul is of Greek origin. To the Hebrews salvation meant the salvation of the people as a whole. Attempts are made to find the germs of belief in immortality in Ezekiel, but generally speaking no belief in personal immortality is to be found in the prophets. In eschatology there is a distinction between the messianic-historical outlook and that of personal immortality. Both the one and the other enter into Christianity. The teaching of ancient Hebrew religion was of a hopeless state, called Sheol, after death, and it believed in the bestowal of rewards in this life only. The Book of Job points to a profound crisis in thought. It was only in the second century that Judaism accepted the belief in recompense in the life to come. But the Hebrews, as distinct from the Greeks, arrived at belief in resurrection with the body, not in the immortality of the soul. It was only the Essenes who took a spiritualistic line and saw in matter the source of evil. Philo, who belongs to Hellenistic thought, expressed not so much the idea of messianic expectation which was concerned with the whole people, as individual expectation in relation to the soul. The gnostics thought that the spiritual element in man must be separated from matter and united with God, who is not the creator of the world.[1] But both Judaism and Hellenism found a solution of the problem of victory over death and the winning of immortality.

It is very interesting to follow the history of the fight for the immortality of the soul among the Greeks.[2] In Homer there is in man an invisible reflection which is set free at death. This is the Psyche. The name remains after death. Homeric religion includes a rational element. In Hesoid people become demons. To attain immortality means to become a god. Immortality is the manifestation in man of the divine principle, and that only is immortal. Man must ward off dangers which threaten him from the chthonic gods, gods of the underground, by the way of purification. Fear of the impure was characteristic of ancient peoples. But the heroes were akin to the chthonic gods and to the dead. The heroes were demi-gods. It was only the heroes, the demigods, not ordinary people, who were immortal. There is a separation between man and the divine race; there is no god-man link. Belief in the immortality of the soul issued from the cult of Dionysus. There was a mingling of the super-human and the inhuman, and the human disappears. And this reappears in Nietzsche, at a much later period of history. Man is mortal. But immortality is possible because there is a divine principle in man. There is a titanic and dionysian element in him. The purely Greek religion of Apollo infiltrated into the elemental dionysian cult,

[1] See Hans Leisegang, *Die Gnosis*, and de Faye, *Gnostiques et Gnosticisme*.
[2] See Rhode's remarkable book, *Psyche*.

and hence Orphism came to birth. The liberation of man comes about not from man himself but by the grace of a saving god. The suffering God gives immortality to man by His death and resurrection. By initiation in the Orphic mysteries the immortality of the soul was bestowed. The dionysian ecstasy frees the god from connection with the body. Heraclitus teaches that the soul is fire. The god is in man; there is no individual immortality; there is only the universal fire. Pythagoras believed in the immortality of the soul, but he connected it with reincarnation. According to Anaxagoras it is the spirit, not the soul which is immortal. The common is immortal, but not the individual. It is difficult to combine the doctrine of individual immortality with the platonic doctrine of ideas. The idea of a world beyond was alien to Greek tragedy. The idea that the soul is immortal in its own nature was alien to popular Greek belief. That idea was developed in theology and philosophy. The quest for immortality was connected with the mysteries, and this indicated the end of tribal religions, and the beginning of universalism.

The difficulty of solving the problem of immortality is due to the fact that it is posed within the perspective of objectivization, of the projection of human existence into the objective world. Externally the soul depends upon the body and the body depends upon the objective physical world. Man is turned into an object, into one of all the many things there are in the world. Biologically death happens from the disintegration of the complex composition of an organism. But the cell, on the other hand is immortal because it is simple. Weismann thought that the germ plasm is virtually immortal. Plato defended the possibility of immortality on the ground that the soul is simple; this became a classical argument for all that it is essentially naturalistic in character. The physical energy of the human organism does not perish, it is only transformed and dissipated in the world. It is permissible to enquire what happens after death to psychical energy. The human organism is a multiple composition; it is colonial and, therefore, easily dissolved. Personality is the unique and unchangeable amid the constant changes of the multiple composition of man; and the spiritual principle is what maintains this uniqueness and this permanence.

But there is a paradox in the fact that the spiritual principle itself requires death, for the infinite aspirations of man are not capable of realization within the bounds of this phenomenal world. Death reigns only in the world of phenomena, which are subject to cosmic and historical time. In existential time it represents merely an experience, only the passing through a test. Death belongs to the destiny of man; to die is to pass through the most irrational, and the most stupendous experience man has.

The spiritual meaning of death is different from the biological meaning. It is a mistake to think that *le néant* exists in the natural world. In nature there is no nothingness, no non-existence; there is only change, dissolution, composition, development. The horror of nothingness, of the abyss of non-being only exists in relation to the spiritual world. Death which reigns in nature is not *le néant*. The horror of death is spiritual, just as the victory over death is spiritual. Death appears quite differently and has an entirely different meaning, when it is looked at from the inward point of view, from the existential point of view, when man does not think of himself as projected into the external object world. In the perspective of interior existence no-one in actual fact recognizes the possibility of the final disappearance of his own ego, of that which has been won as personality. I catch myself in such a contradictory judgment as this: if there is to be nothing for me after death I shall after death be aware of this. If I die and there is to be no further life for me, I finally disappear, and then there will be nothing at all; there will be no world for I was the only proof of the existence of the world.

Human personality is more real than the whole world; it is a noumen as opposed to phenomena; in its kernel it belongs to eternity. But this is not seen from without; it is only seen from within. The human soul is limited by the body; it is dependent upon natural necessity; but inwardly it is infinite. Not only that which at this moment reveals itself as my soul, but also that which reveals itself as my soul throughout the whole extent of my life, is but a small part of my soul as potential infinity both in the direction of light and in the direction of darkness. Life from birth to death is only a tiny fragment of my eternal destiny. What is of vital interest for me is the problem of individuality in me, not the racial in me, nor the impersonal good, nor reason, and so on. If I in my final destiny am fused with God, and my individual ego disappears, then *I* never know this, and it adds nothing to me, for there would be no consciousness of mine to be aware of it. The teaching of Averroes, for instance, about the immortality of the intellect, concerns the immortality of the racial in man; it gives no answer at all to the problem of immortality. The same is true of impersonal racial immortality in the memory of descendants, in ideas, or in created work; they do not solve the problem. Man seeks personal immortality; not immortality in the object, but immortality in the subject. But doctrines of immortality to a large extent bear the marks of objectivization. It is very important to recognize the fact that only the eternal is real. Everything which is not eternal, everything which is transitory, has no true reality. Nietzsche says that eternity was necessary for joy, for the happiness of the moment, and everything is justified. But this only makes sense if that moment itself enters into eternity, and is not a fractional part of time. Nietzsche wrote to Deussen that he would like to be right not just for to-day and for to-morrow but for thousands of years. But there is very little difference between a thousand years and to-day or to-morrow; one must be right for eternity. There is a moment of creative ecstasy and union with God which is communion with eternity and escape from the power of time.

Death, which happens as the outcome of the rhythmic regularity of nature, and to which man is condemned by a biological process, is a most individual and personal thing for man. It means above all the sundering of contacts and relations with other people and with the life of the cosmos. Every man must pass through the tragedy of death. According to Freud death is the goal towards which all life moves; the instinct of the ego is the instinct of death. Yet at the same time, and again according to Freud, who knows nothing of a higher principle in man, nobody believes in his own death. The paradox of death is that although death is the most terrible of evils, one which more than any other arouses fear in men, yet through this evil there is opened up the way to eternal life, or at least one of the ways. Our life is full of paradoxes of this kind. Thus, for instance, war is a very terrible evil, but it may reveal the possibilities of heroism and of rising above the banality of everyday life. A sorry infinity of life is just what would make man a finite creature.

There is a conflict between personal immortality and the begetting of children, which is racial immortality.[1] The power of producing offspring by no means corresponds to the quality of personality; the reverse is rather the case. The most finished individuality may possess the least strength for the production of new lives. Immortality in racial life, in children and grandchildren, like immortality in the nation, in the State, or in the social collective, has nothing in common with the immortality of man. This is true, although in a different degree, not only in regard to the human world but in regard to the animal world also. The relation between personality and sex is very complex and mysterious. Sex is the impersonal, the racial in man: and this distinguishes it from eros which is personal in character. On the one hand sexual energy is an impediment in the struggle for personality and spiritualization, it crushes man beneath its natural

[1] See Solovëv's admirable essay, *The Meaning of Love* (Bles).

featureless impersonality; while, on the other hand, it can be switched over into creative energy, and creative energy requires that man should not be a sexless creature. But the real transfiguration and illumination of man requires victory over sex, which is a mark of the Fall of man. A change of human consciousness is also associated with victory over sex. Immortality is dependant upon the condition of consciousness. It is not a divided consciousness, not one which is disintegrating into its elements or being recomposed from its elements, which leads to immortality, but only an integral consciousness. The immortal in man is also connected with memory. The painful thing in human life is not only forgetfulness of what is precious and dear, loss of a memory; but also, and this is a still more painful thing, the impossibility of forgetting what was evil and grievous in the past. Immortality is memory made clear and serene. The most dreadful thing in life is the sense of irrevocability, of irreparability, of absolute loss. Human freedom can do nothing about this, and belief in natural immortality does not help. This is the point where the divine-human link is broken. It is Godforsakenness. It is only belief in the gracious power which comes from Christ which can help, for in Him the divine-human link is incarnate. Light may be kindled in the most inspissated darkness.

Man aspires to integral immortality, not to the immortality of the superman, or of the intellect, or of the ideal principle in him; he aspires to the immortality of the personal, not of the impersonal and the common. The problem of death has been associated with the problem of sleep. Fechner thinks that death is the transition from the half-sleep which is our earthly life, to awakening and a state of vigilance.[1] A dream indicates the loss of mental synthesis; what Fechner says means that we are still living in a semi-conscious, half-dreaming state. Immortality then will be the transition to full consciousness, which I prefer to call super-consciousness. A

[1] See Fechner, *Das Büchlein vom Leben nach dem Tode.*

full integral consciousness is super-consciousness, and this is also a spiritual awakening. Consciousness which is directed to the phenomenal world is semi-consciousness; it is only the liberation of consciousness from the sole power of the phenomenal world which opens out the prospect of immortality. The terrible thing is that eschatological prospects have been in the majority of cases nightmares, and have revealed the dreadful dejection and terror which are in man.

Human consciousness is subject to many eschatological nightmares, though sometimes they take a beautiful form. Christianity has not to this day overcome the nightmarish character of its personal eschatology. The introduction of the moral principle into beliefs about life beyond the grave was, of course, some progress; it was a spiritualization of magical beliefs. But the moral principle has assumed a character which primarily threatens judgment and instils fear. Even Christian beliefs about the life after death bear the impress of a sadistic imagination; the imagination which has created pictures of life beyond the tomb has been a vindictive and evil imagination. A vengeful apocalypse is already to be found in the Book of Enoch which anticipated the Christian apocalypse. Orphism was a lofty form of Greek religious consciousness; but the idea of hell, of rewards and punishments comes, it would appear, from Orphism.[1] The eschatological nightmares created by man himself, sometimes in a state of fright, sometimes with a desire for vengeance, have taken very different forms. Such nightmares and the prospect of the final disappearance of the whole man, are those of a being who regards himself as the existential centre of the universe, as a greater reality than the reality of the world. The man of our own time who professes naïve materialistic views congruous with his condition of being unawakened spiritually, is obliged to come to terms with these nightmares. And he even contrives to persuade himself that such an eschatolo-

[1] See A. Boulanger, *Orphée*.

gical outlook is a consolation for his earthly life. In actual fact life in such case loses all meaning.

But there are other and more positive views of the future which are no less nightmares, the prospect of endless reincarnation, the prospect of complete loss of personality in an impersonal featureless divinity, and, most of all, the prospect of the eternal pains of hell. And if one could believe in the possibility of endless existence in the conditions of our life, which often make one think of hell, that also would be a nightmare and evoke a desire for death. Indian religious philosophy has regarded reincarnation in a way which differs from that of modern European theosophies. Among the latter it has become an optimistic evolutionary doctrine; whereas among the Indians, it has been a pessimistic belief. Buddhism teaches, above all, the ways of emancipation from the sufferings which belong to reincarnation. Belief in reincarnation is not a beneficent thing, and it provides no liberation from *Karma*. It contains no indication of any way out; it provides no way of issuing out of time into eternity. In addition to which the doctrine of reincarnation justifies social injustice and the caste system. Aurobindo, of whom I have already spoken, constructs a mystical pantheistic doctrine of immortality which is far superior to the theosophical doctrines of reincarnation. According to him death is the answer of the all, the whole, to the false limitation of the ego in its individual form.[1] Aurobindo has also assimilated some Christian elements, but nevertheless he has not the Christian idea of personality. He says that the man who submits to grief and pain, who is the slave of sensations and emotions, who is occupied with ephemeral things, has no knowledge of immortality. He means by this that immortality is something to be won.

The views of Leo Tolstoy on immortality are of a pantheistic character and remind one more of Indian religious philosophy

[1] See Aurobindo, *Upanishad*, cited above.

than of Christianity.[1] He regards the personal life as a false sort of life and in his view personality cannot inherit immortality. The horror of death which caused so much suffering to Tolstoy was connected with his conception of personality, that is to say with a false sort of life. There is no death, he thought, when personal life is overcome. Nietzsche's teaching about the eternal return is the ancient Greek idea which knows only cosmic time and hands man over as a whole into the power of the cosmic cycle. This belongs to the same type of nightmare as the idea of endless reincarnation. The eternal return contradicts another of Nietzsche's ideas, his messianic idea of the superman. About this latter notion I have already written enough. The human, according to Nietzsche, is not only mortal and bound to disappear but its disappearance is even to be desired. Nietzsche's thought is decidedly anti-personalist and so is the idea of his antithesis, Tolstoy.

The teaching of N. Fedorov about resuscitation is the most personalist and human, really human, in character.[2] He demands that all the dead who have preceded us should have life returned to them; he will not acquiesce in regarding any single one of those who have died in the past, as a means to assure the interests of the future or the triumph of any kind of impersonal objective principles whatever, and what is in question is the resuscitation of the whole man. This is not to be a passive expectation of the resurrection of the dead but a process which involves active participation, that is to say an act of resuscitation, reanimation. But the philosophical weakness of Fedorov lay in this, that he laid too little stress upon the creative power of the spirit in the resuscitation of the dead, and placed too much faith in the power of technical knowledge. And in this the influence of an age of scientific naturalism makes itself felt. Fedorov is absolutely right in seeing that the principal thing in Christianity is not justification, but

[1] See Tolstoy's book, *Concerning Life*.
[2] See N. Fedorov, *The Philosophy of the Common Task*.

immortalization, the acquisition of immortality, not the justification of it.

The need of immortality lies in the very depths of human nature. But the beliefs in immortality carry the impress of the limitation of human nature. Into them there enter also the evil human instincts which have created pictures of paradise and, especially, of hell. It has been most difficult of all to speak about paradise, for in spite of everything, hell was nearer to man; there was less of the other world about it. But the picture of paradise so easily gave rise to boredom. The subject of paradise greatly disturbed Dostoyevsky, and he gave expression to some remarkable thoughts about it; for instance, in *The Dream of the Ridiculous Man*. He always connected the subject of paradise with the subject of freedom; he could not accept paradise apart from freedom; but at the same time freedom might create hell too. The repellant character of the picture of a paradise which bears, by transference, the sensual marks of this world, in which the righteous even take pleasure in the suffering of sinners in hell, is due to the fact that nothing could be less apophatic than the way in which people were thinking about paradise. For kataphatic thought about paradise will always be intolerable to the more refined moral and aesthetic sense. Life is throughout infinite; but kataphatic thought about paradise has a finitude which is devoid of true creative life. Jaspers is fond of speaking about the *frontier-position* of man (*Grenzsituation*),[1] and in truth man finds himself on the boundary lines of various worlds; he is not present as a whole in one world only. Man is a being of many planes; at one time he is transported to the other world; at another he touches the edge of the abyss.

The metaphysical problem of immortality is connected most of all with the problem of time. Is his existence in this cosmic and historical time the only existence of man? Or does he exist in existential time as well, which comes into touch with eternity and

[1] See K. Jaspers, *Philosophie*.

plunges man into eternity? To deny immortality is to make the assumption that his existence in time is the final and only one; it is to say that he is crushed by time and the phenomenal world. The last word in the philosophy which Heidegger, as up to the present propounded, is the finite character of human existence. *Dasein* which with him replaces the real man is finite existence moving towards death. The nightmare idea of hell was due to a confusion between eternity and infinity. But the idea of an eternal hell is absolutely absurd. Hell is not eternity; there is no other sort of eternity than divine eternity. Hell is an evil infinitude, the impossibility of issuing out of time into eternity; it is a nightmare phantom born of the objectivization of human existence, which is submerged in the time of our æon. If there were such a thing as an eternal hell it would be the final failure and defeat of God; and the condemnation of the creation of the world as a diabolical farce.[1] But there are many, many Christians to whom hell is very dear, though not for themselves, of course. The ontology of hell is the most evil form of objectivization, the most pretentiously exacting, the most inspired by feelings of vengeance and malice. But the psychology of hell is possible, and is associated with a real experience.

The legal interpretation of immortality is as base as the ancient magical conception. There is an educational element which plays a very large part in the traditional doctrines of immortality, and this is clearly of an exoteric character. Only a spiritual conception of immortality answers to the higher consciousness, but the spiritual conception by no means indicates that it is only the spiritual part of man which is immortal. The resurrection of the body must also be understood in a spiritual sense. 'It is sown a natural body; it is raised a spiritual body.' Man is immortal because the divine principle is in him, but it is not only the divine in man which is immortal; it is the whole organism of man of which the spirit has

[1] On this subject there are many admirable ideas in S. Bulgakov. See his *Bride of the Lamb*; this is the third part of his theological system.

taken possession, which is immortal. It is the spiritual in man which also battles against the final objectivization of human existence, the definitive objectivization which issues in death for man by submerging him finally in the death-dealing stream of time. The objectivization of consciousness produces the illusion of an objective spirit which knows of immortality as impersonal only.

An intense consciousness of one's own vocation and one's mission in the world may bestow the sense of immortality, and that independently of a man's conscious ideas. Then there occurs an interlacement of personal eschatology and the historical eschatology of the whole world. My immortality cannot be separated from the immortality of other people and of the world. To be absorbed exclusively in one's own personal immortality or with one's personal salvation is transcendent egoism. If the idea of personal immortality is separated from the universal eschatological outlook, from the destiny of the world, it becomes a contradiction of love. But love is the principal spiritual weapon in the fight against the sovereignity of death. These two antitheses, love and death, are linked together. Love is revealed at its greatest strength when death is near, and love cannot but conquer death. He who truly loves is the conqueror of death. We ought to make superhuman efforts to secure that those whom we love—not only people but animals too—should inherit eternal life. Christ conquered death because He was the incarnation of the universal divine love and love cannot fail to desire universal salvation from death, and universal resurrection. Were there to be but one creature possessing an existential centre, which was not resuscitated to eternal life, the world would have been a failure and a theodicy would be impossible. In such conditions my personal immortality would not only be lacking in some respect; it would, in fact, be impossible. I depend upon the destiny of the world and of those who are near to me, and the destiny of those who are near to me and of the world depends upon me.

Fedorov was right and proclaimed a sacred truth when he demanded that man should be an agent of resurrection, but he bound the destiny of man too exclusively with this phenomenal world, with this present scheme of existence. The death of a man in this earthly scheme of existence cannot be finally decisive for his destiny. If reincarnation in a single scheme of existence clashes with the idea of personality, reincarnation in a multiple scheme of existence is entirely compatible with the idea of personality. The fact that the path by which human life attains the realization of fullness of life, takes its way through the spiritual world, is not in the least a contradiction of the truth that the human body, the form of the body, and not just the soul alone, must inherit eternity. For the fact that the form of the body is indissolubly linked with the image of human personality certainly does not mean an indissoluble link with the material of the body, which in its physical-chemical composition is essentially mortal. The resurrection of the body is the resurrection of the spiritual body.

The most mysterious of links is the link between personal destiny and historical messianism. The fullness of Christian truth which can be realized only in a religion of the spirit, involves the union of personal immortality with the messianic solution of the destiny of history, of the mystical idea with the prophetic idea. Both the way of spiritual life which seeks the highest in withdrawal from the destinies of the world and history and is unwilling to share in them, and on the other hand the way which pursues the same end by exclusive attention to the destinies of history, society and the world, and forsakes the personal spiritual path, both these are alike incomplete and mistaken in their exclusiveness. In this lies the whole complexity of the problem of immortality. Immortality is not simply a human achievement, nor is it merely a divine gift, it is a divine-human enterprise; it is the task of freedom and a work of grace, immortality is an effect which is accomplished both from below and from above. It is loose thinking to suppose that man is by nature an immortal being, neither is it accurate to think that he merely receives his immortality from above, from the divine power.

The mistake here, as everywhere, lies in the rupture of the link which binds the human and the divine together, in the self-assertion of man and at the same time in the degradation of man, of his true humanity. At every turn we are apt to find ourselves thinking of immortality by transferring to the phenomenal world that which is relevant only to the noumenal world and by transferring to the noumenal world that which is relevant only to the phenomenal world. We also think mistakenly when we make an absolute break between the phenomenal world and the noumenal world. The doctrine of immortality must pass through the cleansing flame of criticism, just as the doctrine of revelation also must pass through it. They must be purified from naïve anthropomorphism, cosmomorphism, and sociomorphism. But there is a true anthropomorphism which issues from the central position which man occupies and from the fact of commensurability between the human and the divine. This anthropomorphism ought to be united with theomorphism, that is to say it ought to be divine-human. The true vista of immortality is at once human and divine, and not abstractly human. Thus in the problem of immortality we again meet with the same dialectic of the divine and the human.

CHAPTER XII

Messianism and History

It is not only upon interpretation of the meaning of history, but also upon the formation of the very category of the historical, that messianism has its bearing. History is created by the expectation that in the future there will be a great manifestation, and that this manifestation will be a disclosure of Meaning in the life of the nations. It is the expectation of the appearance of the Messiah or of the messianic kingdom. The movement of history is also a movement towards that messianic appearance which will bring with it liberation from slavery and suffering, which will inaugurate for man a state of happiness. Messianic consciousness is born in suffering. When suffering does not crush man it is changed into a terrible power. The dynamic messianic myth is turned towards the future. It is in this respect a contrast to pagan myths, which were turned not towards the future but to the past.[1] It was characteristic of the Greeks to be concerned with the contemplation of the cosmos and its cyclic movement. This postulates that the world is eternal and has neither beginning nor end, a world, above all, in space and not a world in time. No philosophy of history is to be found either in Plato or in Aristotle. It is in ancient Israel that the philosophy of history begins, in the revelation of God in history, which found expression in the consciousness of the prophets, and in the Book of Daniel. But a philosophy of history becomes finally possible only in Christianity.[2] The

[1] There are some interesting ideas in this connection in Tillich, *Die sozialistische Entscheidung*.

[2] This is the opinion of Dilthey also, though as a matter of fact he himself denies the possibility of a philosophy of history. See his *Einleitung in die Geistes-Wissenschaften*.

ancient sage attained inward peace, harmony and joy without being concerned with any change in the world, without asking for any historical movement in it, and with no disquietude about the future. Christianity introduced disquietude about the future, a messianic and eschatological disquietude. For that reason it requires change and movement, and postulates hope. The origins of Christian messianism are ancient Hebrew and perhaps Persian, but it is not derived from Greece. For Christian thought time and history acquire a metaphysical meaning; and this would have been entirely incomprehensible to Plato and Plotinus. Christian metaphysics are not an ontology, although efforts have been made to find a basis for it in Greek philosophy, it is above all a philosophy of history, it is messianic and prophetic. Primitive Christianity lived by hope, the hope of the appearance of the Son of Man in glory. The first Christians believed that the prophetic gifts of the Spirit would continue to exist until the Second Coming of Christ. This attitude to history is a paradox. On the one hand a tense expectation of the speedy manifestation of Christ and the messianic kingdom, the expectation of the coming of the end, obscured the long drawn-out vista of history. But, on the other hand, this tense eschatological expectation also gave a meaning to history, in interpreting it as a movement towards the Kingdom of God. If the historical process is regarded as endless, history is deprived of meaning, and is drawn into the cosmic process with its cyclic movement. The philosophy of history is always prophetic and cannot be otherwise. History has not yet reached its end, and the historical philosopher finds himself in the midst of the historical process. How is it possible to understand the meaning of history without knowing what the last stage of history will be like? It is on this ground that the possibility of a philosophy of history has been denied. It is evident that a philosophy of history cannot be scientific; it can only be prophetic. It postulates the vision of a light which streams from the future; and it is only this light which proclaims a meaning for history.

History has a meaning only if it is going to come to an end; its having a meaning depends upon its not going on for ever. History has no immanent meaning; it has only a transcendent meaning, and it is the messianic consciousness which proclaims this transcendent meaning for it. From the immanent point of view history is a failure and has no meaning. The soil of history is volcanic, and the volcanic explosions tell of contact with the end and of the possibility of a messianic consummation of history. The attempt to construct a naturalistic philosophy of history, which permits its subordination to the cosmic process, as a part of that process, gives no meaning at all to history. On the contrary it is not history that is part of the cosmic process, but the cosmic process which is part of history. It is in the history of man, not in the history of nature, that the meaning of the world is hidden. The whole religious consciousness of paganism was steeped in the cosmos and in cosmic time. It was on that soil that the naturalistic myths grew up, with their concern for the past, and their opposition to prophetic and messianic consciousness. Prophetism is opposed to that political romanticism which idealizes the past. Among the peoples generally referred to as pagan it was the Persians alone whose religious thought was able to give a meaning to history, and that was because it recognized an apocalypsis of the end, and in that way it influenced Hebrew religion also. Without prophetism Christianity would have no relation to history; it would have no future; it is only from the future that light can be thrown upon the past.

The prophetic character of the philosophy of history may take secularized forms; it was so in the thought of the nineteenth century. Kant says '*Die Philosophie könne auch ihren Chiliasmus haben*'.[1]

[1] Kant's *Populäre Schriften:* '*Idee zu einer allgemeinen Geschichte in Weltburgerlicher Ansicht.*

This chiliasm, that is to say the messianic idea, is deeply inherent in all the philosophy of history which belongs to the nineteenth century, though it had to all appearances broken away from Christianity. The prophetic element in that philosophy of history was stronger than in the religious philosophy of history of St Augustine and Bossuet. This can be said of Hegel, Marx, St Simon and Comte. The whole of their philosophy of history was permeated by prophetism and has no meaning without it. It is not less prophetic in Comte and Marx who were opponents of metaphysics, than in Hegel, the metaphysician. Hegel recognized a goal of world history. In it the world spirit is finally to arrive at self-consciousness through man. History is a progressive growth in the consciousness of freedom and in the actual realization of the reign of freedom. Comte knows that in the history of mankind a positive period will come to replace the theological and metaphysical period, and that the religion of humanity will triumph. Karl Marx knows that in place of the bourgeois capitalist period marked by the exploitation and slavery of man there will come a period in which socialism will be triumphant, when the messianic class, the proletariat, to which the properties of the chosen people of God were transferred, will realize justice in the world and liberate not only itself but all mankind.

Whence comes this knowledge of the mankind of the future? Is it possible to regard it as scientific knowledge? No, it is messianic faith; it is a secularized form of the old chiliastic idea. The idea of the progress of mankind, which since the time of Condorcet has been fundamental to the philosophy of history, is religious and Christian in its origin; it is a secularized form of the Christian idea of movement towards the Kingdom of God as the basic theme of world history. The idea of progress seeks to give a meaning to world history but its exponents are under the illusion that it gives an immanent meaning to history whereas in fact its meaning is transcendent. The idea of progress must be distinguished from the idea of evolution which is scientific and biological in its origin. There is a fundamental inconsistency in the doctrine of progress and it lies in the fact that every human generation and every human personality is thought of as a means to serve the interests of following generations, of perfection which lies in the future, of the Kingdom of God on earth, into which will enter those happy ones who live in time to come, but not all those generations of the dead; they will have been turned into a mere means to an end. The doctrine of progress is anti-personalist. But it is permeated with the messianic idea. the roots and sources of which are religious in character. Without the messianic idea, history becomes a mass of facts heaped together and without any meaning in their connection.[1]

But the messianic idea by no means implies an optimistic view of history. On the contrary it involves a tragic view of history. History is a struggle of opposed principles and not everything in it comes to a successful issue. Not only does good accumulate in it but evil also and for that reason history will have to have an end. But the Kingdom of God will come to a successful issue and in it all the oppositions and conflicts between the two worlds will be resolved. The coming of the thousand years' reign can be thought of only antithetically, it must be regarded as belonging both to the here and now, and to the world beyond, as at the same time earthly and heavenly. There is in history no continuous operation of the providence of God as the incarnation and development of spirit, as Hegel taught; there are only inrushes. The freedom of man also operates in history and so does fate. Chance operates in it also, and chance is rationally inexplicable.[2] Future perfection is a phenomenon which belongs to the transcendent order, but the transcendent can become immanent. The old antithesis between

[1] In this connection there is an interesting book by Theodore Lessing, *Geschichte als Sinngebung des Sinnlosen.*

[2] See Fabre d'Olivet, *Histoire Philosophique du genre humaine.*

the immanent and the transcendent is out of date. Without prophetism, which has been so much enfeebled in historical Christianity, Christianity would have no relation to history. Since historical Christianity has lost the prophetic spirit it cannot understand the meaning of history. That meaning is revealed only to eschatological Christianity. The denial of the possibility of a Christian messianism is a reactionary tendency in Christianity.[1] Messianism is a prophetic premonition not only of the Second Coming of the Messiah, but also of the messianic Kingdom. Christianity is a messianic, prophetic religion, which looks towards the future, towards the Kingdom of God. Light comes not only from the past; light comes also from the future. It stands to reason that there is always a danger of false messianism and of false messiahs. As instances of false messianism one might mention such cases as that of Thomas Müntzer. But the case of Joachim of Floris was not false messianism, it was messianism which was premature, and come before its time.

It is untrue to think that after the coming of Christ the Messiah, the Kingdom of God had definitely come and there was nothing further to wait for in the future; that from that time messianism lost all its *raison d'être*. There is a similar way of thinking, turned exclusively to the past, which is based on a false identification of the Kingdom of God with the Church. That was what St Augustine taught and this opinion of his has become dominant in Roman Catholicism. In this way the authority of the historical Church has been strengthened and the possibility of any prophetism has been warded off. Expectations which are turned towards the future are regarded as dangerous; and it is preferred not to speak about the second appearance of Christ the Messiah. The Apocalypse is hushed up. This attitude exists in Orthodoxy also, though it is less marked there than in Roman Catholicism, which is more highly

[1] See Féret, *L'Apocalypse de St Jean. Vision chrétienne de l'histoire*. The book has many good qualities but Christian messianism is decisively repudiated in it.

organized. But after all the Gospel is the good news of the coming of the Kingdom of God; and the very idea of the Kingdom of God is an eschatological idea.[1] We pray 'Thy kingdom come'; and that means that the Kingdom of God has not yet come, although the Church has already existed for some two thousand years. The Church is simply the path of history, and not the actual appearance of the Kingdom of God. The Church is one separate phenomenon in this historical life of peoples and not the total phenomenon that the Kingdom of God must be. The Church is not the transfiguration of the world. The future Kingdom of God is only symbolically established in it. I am speaking of the historical, not of the mystical Church. Such is the most important fact in the historical destiny of Christianity.

Christ in His preaching proclaimed the near approach of the Kingdom of God, that is to say of a completely new world and a new life. The first Christians lived in an eschatological atmosphere; they were waiting for the second appearance of Christ, for the end of this world and the coming of the promised Kingdom of God. But they did not see the long path of history which lies between the two comings of Christ, and their expectations were not justified by the course of events. Christ has not come upon earth for the second time; the last times have not arrived. The long pathway of history has been revealed, and on this long path, instead of the Kingdom of God, the Church had to appear and to organize itself in the same way as great historical bodies always organize themselves. It was the Church upon this earth which came, instead of the Kingdom of God, and it began to develop in accordance with the conditions of this world. Messianic expectations have been driven inwards and later on have made their appearance again in a secularized form. Prophetism has been more and more stifled and has given rise to suspicions of heresy. Sometimes it appears in a premature and falsely exalted form, as in

[1] See Johannes Weiss, *Die Predigt Jesu vom Reiche Gottes*, and also Loisy's books.

Montanism. The Apostle Paul says (I Cor. XIV. I) 'Desire earnestly spiritual gifts, but rather that ye may prophesy.' These words are repeated with reluctance. Sacramentalism is opposed to messianism, and personal salvation and immortality are opposed to the Kingdom of God.

But the meaning of history between the two comings of Christ must be justified, and given the complete stifling of the prophetic spirit this meaning cannot be understood. The priest has more and more crowded out the prophet; ritualism is dominant. But ritualism does not confer any understanding whatever of the meaning of history. The enfeeblement of the part played by Christianity in history is explained by this weakening of the messianic consciousness. The prophet listened to the Voice of God, but men have ceased to listen to that divine Voice and it has ceased to be audible. The expectation of a personal messiah was revealed in the Hebrew people, not among its scribes and priests. Judaism turned prophecy into a religion of law and the torah. The same thing has happened in Christianity also. Pharisaism is a phenomenon which belongs not to Hebrew religion only but also to the Christian religion, with this difference, that after the Coming of Christ pharisaism became much worse. The cooling of the fire of the original revelation, the reign of law, of formalism and of pharisaism, are phenomena which are repeated in all religions. It has been the case in Judaism, in Buddhism, in Islam and in Christianity. The painful side of the problem of messianism and history is that man cannot for the sake of the messianic idea throw off the burden of history and refuse to take it on himself; he is obliged to submit to the heavy labours which history thrusts upon him. Dreamy messianism is a false frame of mind. Here we are confronted by a paradox. The messianic consciousness and expectation creates history, proclaims a meaning for it and holds it together, and yet at the same time it, so to speak, breaks down history and seeks to overleap it. This contradiction has to be accepted as a part of experience.

In the same way as the first Coming of the Messiah was prepared among the Hebrew people, so now among all mankind the way must be prepared for the Second Coming; and it is in this that history has its justification. The goal is no less than the attainment of the creative fullness of life and the realization of the Spirit not only in human life but also in the life of the cosmos.

It is possible to distinguish four types of messianism according to their various characteristics: (1) national or universal messianism; (2) messianism which is concerned with this world or with the next; (3) victorious or suffering messianism, and (4) messianism which is personal or impersonal. All these types were already to be met with in Israel. In Egypt there was messianism associated with the divine nature of the king. The messiah means in the first place God's Anointed, and the messianic idea of the king as the Anointed One is preserved also in Christianity, although it has nothing in common with Christianity. Messianism is always connected with millenarianism, with the expectation of the thousand years' reign. The messianism of the nineteenth and twentieth centuries, secularized and torn away from its religious roots, also awaits a thousand years' reign, and this is true of Hegel, Marx, Comte and even of German racism. But this secularized messianism is commonly of this world, triumphant and impersonal. In this connection there are, according to Hegel, three periods of history to be noted, the period of thesis, of antithesis and of synthesis. In the third period there should come the perfect order, the triumph of freedom, the triumph of reason and science, the triumph of justice, and universal happiness. This hope of the inauguration of the perfect order in the third period, this hope of attaining the summit of progress, is a messianic hope; it is the expectation of the thousand years' reign. Science can have nothing to say about this.

In the past the clearest manifestation of religious messianism was the case of Joachim of Floris in the thirteenth century, who looked for the coming of the third epoch of the Holy Spirit, and the religious movement in Italy during that period. In the nineteenth century messianism at times assumed religious and prophetic forms, and at other times forms which externally were anti-religious. Messianism and prophetism are to be traced in St Simon, Fourier, de Maistre (the expectation of a new revelation of the Holy Spirit), in Comte, Hegel and Schelling (Johannine Christianity), in Cieszkowski (the most remarkable of them), in Marx, in Nietzsche (the coming of the superman, and the Dionysiac culture), in Ibsen (the third kingdom), and in the apocalyptic Léon Bloy. Among the Russians it is to be seen in Dostoyevsky, Vladimir Solovëv, N. Fedorov and even in the Russian socialists and anarchists, and especially in the religious anarchism of Tolstoy. Expectation is always associated with messianism, the expectation which faces the future, but an expectation which is not passive but active, and which makes an appeal for action. It is activity in history but it is inspired by belief in the coming of the end of history. To this is due the apparent inconsistency of the messianic consciousness.

In our day it is only the Russians and the Germans who have had a philosophy of history. The German philosophy of history is pantheistic and cosmic; the Russian philosophy of history is divine-human and eschatological. But both the one people and the other are inspired by messianic passion, and it is this that determines their dynamism and activism. This dynamism and activity would be impossible given a purely spiritual interpretation of the Kingdom of God and a purely individualistic conception of immortality. A messianic attitude of mind is essential for the solution of world history, and messianism as a religious phenomenon is bound up with the prophetic side of religion. A purely sacramental interpretation of religion is not favourable to the prophetic spirit and to messianic expectation. There is in that case no belief that light issues not only from the past but shines also from the future. And prophetism is a principle which leads to rebirth, to a new life. It is not true that the prophet is merely a passive instrument in the hand of God. In prophetism humanity too is in the highest degree active; prophecy is a divine-human activity, it is divine-human creativeness. Prophetism in literature, in art, in philosophy, in social movements, is the creative activity of man. It is a fatal mistake to sever God-manhood into two parts and to say that in religion, in the spiritual life, God alone acts, and that in culture, and social life man alone acts. In actual fact the divine-human link holds in both cases. And if there is a dualism, and dualism is necessary to activity and struggle, yet it is a dualism of an entirely different character; it is not the dualism of the divine and the human but the dualism of freedom and necessity, of good and evil.

Three points of view may be taken: (1) the religiously social; this is racial and tribal, it belongs to Judaism and the ancient pagan world; (2) the religiously individualistic; this involves withdrawal from the world and history, e.g. the religion of India, neoplatonism, and Eckhardt; (3) the Christian messianic, which is at the same time spiritual; this rises above the power of the national, racial and State principle. It not only postulates the existence of the transcendent, but also recognizes the possibility of changing our world by means of the transcendent. This third point of view does not admit that ideal spiritual principles are progressively incarnated and defended in history, in the State, in authority, and in the objectivizing of spirit. History is tragedy and in a certain sense tragi-comedy. The activity of man, which is a duty laid upon him, ought not to depend upon success, upon its realization in history. It is admirably said in the *Bhagavad-gita* that one ought not to look for the fruits of an action.[1] Every positive, good act of man will nevertheless have its importance for eternity,

[1] There are some remarkable thoughts about time recorded by St Augustine in his *Confessions*.

for the Kingdom of God, even if the powers of darkness and evil have acted against it and prevented its realization in time.

The philosophy of history raises the problem of the relation of history to time, to freedom and to personality. And these relations present paradoxes. Time is in itself a paradox; the swift movement of time, its break-up into a past, which no longer exists, a future, which does not yet exist, and a present which is in part already past, and in part still belongs to the future, makes it difficult to capture its reality. There is a present of the past, a present of the present and a present of the future. The whole of our life depends upon time, and time brings death to us. Creative acts are accomplished in time; acts which bring newness with them. History takes place in time; but historical time is different from cosmic time. The movement which occurs in historical time is not in a circle, it is not cyclic; it streams out in a forward direction; it is movement which is directed towards a goal. But it is just in historical time that the goal is not attainable, and a sinister infinity is disclosed. An issue is possible only by a break-through of the transcendent. Immanently history may be bent upon the creation of a perfectly rationalized and mechanized society. But I do not want that, I want the Kingdom of God, which cometh not with observation.

The relation of history to freedom is also a paradox. History in which there is a meaning presupposes the existence of freedom. Christianity is historical precisely because freedom is revealed in it. Without freedom there is no history but only the realm of nature. Yet at the same time history suppresses the freedom of man; it subordinates him to its own necessities. It is a notable idea of Hegel's, that the cunning of reason reigns in history and subordinates everything to itself, for the sake of ends which are non-human.[1] Man creates history and packs it with his own creative power. Yet history treats man with indifference and

[1] See Hegel, *Vorlesungen über die Philosophie der Geschichte.*

cruelty; there is a real demonism in history. Man is a historical being and, therefore, he cannot throw off the burden of history.

The greatest paradox of all is to be seen in the relation between personality and history. The conflict of personality and world history is the fundamental conflict in human life. It is men such as Dostoyevsky and Kierkegaard who have been so acutely aware of this. History does not solve the problem of personality and its destiny and, therefore, the end of history is inevitable. People differ greatly according to whether they regard freedom of personality, the Church regarded as a spiritual society, and spiritual communion, as the highest of values, or whether they regard the supreme value as being the power of the State and the nation, and the external hierarchy of the Church. The foes of liberty are actuated by fear, and fear is one of the chief factors in history, as well as one of the signs of the Fall of man. The only thing which raises him up again is the messianic consciousness, the consciousness of aspiration and movement towards the end. And progress itself is twofold in its nature; it may be either orientated to the resolving end, to the Kingdom of God, to the immanent and the transcendent, or it may be an endless process to which there can be no solution, which contains nothing of value in itself and in which everything is turned into a means. It is in this that the inner contradiction of progress consists. It is this that constitutes the inner contradiction of history itself, which both has a meaning and is meaningless, and so reminds one of a comedy; it both moves towards an end, and is at the same time infinite in the bad sense of the word.

And the existence of the Church in history is in the same way just as inconsistent. The historical Church reminds one of other historical bodies, is very similar to the State, to the kingdom of Caesar; for it also shows relativeness, capacity for adaptation, it also is subject to the power of necessity. But the Church is also meta-historical; another world beyond this world is disclosed in it. It is a spiritual society; the realm of freedom is in it, and that is not like the realm of nature. All the complexity and painfulness of the history of the Church is due to this mingling of its two natures. The Church must function within nature and it takes the sins of history upon itself, but since it is meta-historical it ought to lead to the Kingdom of God. There is a profound sense in which it is, as it were, the soul of history and the soul of the cosmos, and its boundaries do not coincide with the visible boundaries of the Church of history. The life of the Church is a process at once divine and human and the human principle plays a double part in it, creatively positive and distortingly negative. There is an inertly conservative immobile principle in it which is hostile to all creative life, it is a human, all too human, principle, and is certainly not divine, as its defenders seek to maintain. All the conflicts and contradictions of history are echoed in the life of the Church. History is a combination of tradition and creative change. Tradition, behind which a real creative life has existed in the past, may turn into mere deadening inertia, it may harden into immobility, and so become a betrayal of its own past, a denial of creative movement. Change ought not to be mere opportunist adjustment to the world taken as we find it, as a *datum*. It is only the messianic consciousness within the Church which is earnestly directed towards the Kingdom of God; in which both religion and the Church disappear as separate forms which have arisen in the course of history.

Everything which is actualized in history gives the impression of failure. What is actually realized is not what was envisaged by the creative ideal. Christianity above all has not turned out well in history. There is a tragic lack of congruity between the Christians of the catacombs and the Christians of papal and imperial grandeur and power, between persecuted Christian and Christians who persecute. All religions have turned out badly. It is ridiculous to say that the French Revolution made freedom, equality and brotherhood a realized fact. There is a shattering lack of correspondence between the revolutionary bolsheviks during the period of underground activity and exile, and the same people at the zenith of their power, with their uniforms and orders, at courts and in embassies and so on. And there is the same incongruity to be noted between the Reformation of Luther and the Lutheran pastors of the nineteenth century. All grandiose schemes of world empire have been of short duration, for example, the Empire of Alexander of Macedonia which disappeared with his death, and the Roman Empire, and the Empire of Charles the Great, and of Napoleon. The glory and majesty of this world are short-lived and unreal. The same thing will happen also in the case of the socialist realm which has been made a realized fact. Power belongs to the prince of this world and he plays malicious tricks upon the projects of human beings. Human societies pass from a state of constraint, oppression, cruelty, and danger, with no guarantee of life and in fear of the horrors of war and revolution, that is to say from a grim and harsh life, to a life which is more peaceful, contented and free, to a life of bourgeois pettiness, to the pursuit of pleasure, and thus to demoralization and decadence; and then the whole process is begun all over again. And so the tragi-comedy of history goes on.

Does this mean that it is necessary to repudiate history entirely? No. History is a test, it is a creative experiment through which man must pass. The failures of history, the failure of all the realizations of history, are not pure loss, it is through the very failures that man moves forward towards the Kingdom of God. This simply leads us on to the problem of the end. The Kingdom of God is not actually realized in the conditions of our world. What is needed for its realization is not changes *in* this world, but a change *of* this world, not a change of time, but victory over time. Messianism is the belief that new times are at hand, that the Kingdom of God is coming, that the Messiah will appear in power. The expectation which inspires the messianic consciousness lies on the frontier of two worlds, on the frontier between this world and the world beyond, between the immanent and the transcendent, between the earthly and the heavenly, on the boundary which divides the historical and the meta-historical. Messianic expectations cannot be realized either within history itself or outside history. This is a contradiction which is embedded in our limited consciousness, in our fallen reason. Every creative act of man is subject to failure in the sense that the created product actually realized is not what was planned in the creative mind. But at the same time every creative act is essentially eschatological in character, in it this world comes to an end and the other world begins. But our limited consciousness does not see this clearly enough.

In the present-day world two messianic ideas have clashed with one another, the Russian and the German. The Russian idea, in its purest form, is the idea of actually realizing the ideals of truth and right, of the brotherhood of men and of peoples. The Russians have inherited this idea. It is inherent in the prophets, in the eternal truths of Christianity, in certain doctors of the Church, particularly the Eastern, and in that quest for truth which is characteristic of the Russian people themselves. The German idea is the idea of dominance by a chosen race, by a race of masters born to rule over other races and peoples, who are regarded as inferior. This idea is the heir of the old pagan idea, the Greco-Roman idea, of the selective formation of a race of lords who are powerful and turn the weak into slaves. The way was prepared for this idea in German thought by a whole series of pan-Germanists.[1] The first idea aspires towards the Kingdom of God; it means the quest for the 'truth about the earth',[2] which has still not been sufficiently brought to light in historical Christianity, and which can be revealed only in the crowning revelation of the Spirit.

[1] See *Le Pangermanisme philosophique. Préface par Ch. Andler.*

[2] A phrase of the apocalyptist and chiliast V. Tarnovtsev, who made use of it in a series of religious philosophical conferences at Petersburg in 1903.

CHAPTER XIII

Religion of the Spirit
A Devout Meditation

The greatest error of which historical Christianity is guilty is due to the circumscribing and deadening notion that revelation is finished and that there is nothing more to be expected, that the structure of the Church has been completely built and that the roof has been put on it. Religious controversy is essentially concerned with the problem of the possibility of a new revelation and of a new spiritual era. All other questions are of secondary importance. The new revelation is certainly not to be thought of as a new religion distinct from Christianity, but as the fulfilment and crowning of the Christian revelation, and the achievement of its true œcumenicity. There is as yet no œcumenicity. The revelation of the Spirit cannot be just simply waited for; it depends also upon the creative activity of man; it cannot be understood simply as a new revelation of God to man; it is also a revelation of man to God. This means that it will be a divine-human revelation. The separation and opposition of the divine and the human will be overcome in the Spirit, although the distinction between them will be preserved. This is the crowning point in the mystical dialectic of the divine and the human. It is also the end of objectivization, of the projection of revelation into the external, and of naïve realism in the conception of revelation.

In the relation between man and God an infinite spiritual experience is possible. It may be thought that the religion of the Spirit—and it is that precisely of which we are speaking—is a new form of immanentism. But the old controversies about immanentism and transcendentism must be regarded as completely out of date. The very way in which the matter was put was entirely wrong, it was abstract and not dialectic. Just as one cannot break the bond between the divine and the human, and affirm one of these principles in the abstract, so we must not make a break between the transcendent and the immanent, and affirm either of them in the abstract. Real life is in the inter-relation between the one and the other. The transcendent becomes immanent and without its immanence it is abstract and lifeless. It is merely objectivization at its limit. And equally the immanent must not be thought of without the transcendent. Life in the immanent postulates a process of transcendence. Pure immanentism which denies the transcendent is continuance in a circle which has no outlet. When the human is looked upon as the divine, and the identity of the two is affirmed, authentic life comes to an end and its dramatic character exists no longer. When the transcendent is thought of exclusively as immanent and there is no transcendent mystery and remoteness, the immanent is deprived of life and content. On these grounds what was known as immanentism in controversies of an earlier day, which are now out of date, ought to be decisively rejected.

The Holy Spirit is the principle of union between God and the creature,[1] and it is in Him that the mystery of creation, a mystery which is anthropological and cosmological must be revealed. The religion of the Spirit, which is also the religion of the Trinity, will not be in the least like E. von Hartmann's monistic religion of the spirit, in which there is nothing Christian whatever.[2] The coming of a new era of the Spirit into which the highest attainments of spirituality will enter, presupposes a change in human consciousness and that it is given a new orientation. It is a revolutionary change in consciousness, which has been hitherto conceived in a static way. Myths, legends, dogmas will appear in a

[1] The Catholic writer Henstenberg writes in an interesting way on this subject, *Das Bund zwischen Gott und Schöpfung*.

[2] E. von Hartmann, *Die Religion des Geistes*.

different light according to the degrees of consciousness, according to the extent to which its immobility and induration have been overcome. The religion of the Spirit will be the religion of man when he has come of age; it will constitute his emergence from childhood and youth.

Certain traits of this eternal religion, which is new only in external appearance, of this Christian and Trinitarian religion, this religion freed from slavery to the world of objects, can be guessed. In the religion of the Spirit, the religion of freedom, everything will appear in a new light. There will be no authority and no retribution; the nightmare of a legalistic conception of Christianity and of an everlasting hell, will finally disappear. It will have as its basis not judgment at a tribunal and retribution, but creative development and transfiguration, assimilation to God. A new anthropology will be revealed and the religious meaning of human creativeness will be recognized. It will be understood that freedom is its primary basis. The idea of God will be purified from servile sociomorphism. The idea of God as sufficient unto Himself and as a potentate who wields power, still includes relics of an idolatry which is not yet overcome. It is only the conception of God as suffering, and yearning for the Other, and as sacrificed, which subdues atheism and the fight against God. There is a paradox in the knowledge of God which must be courageously faced and put into words, thus; the affirmation of God by my whole being means that God exists; human freedom creates God, and this means that God is; my creating of God is a divine-human act of creation.

All this leads to a revaluation of the idea of Providence, a matter with which atheism is more closely connected than with anything else. The religion of the Spirit is the expectation that a new community of mankind will be revealed, a sense of communion of spirit which is really human, one which radiates kindness and love. The religion of the Spirit is also the expectation of the revelation of a new relation between man and the cosmos, and an expectation of the transfiguration of the cosmos. The process of the disintegration of the cosmos which is due to a merely scientific and technical relation to it, is coming to an end. Its final phase will be the disintegration of the atom. All this finds support in the subject of eschatology, in an active view of eschatology. But in no degree whatever does it mean an optimistic conception of history. Of this I have already spoken. The revelation of light in no sense means the denial of darkness. On the contrary, before the coming of the era of the Spirit, man will have to pass through a thickening of the darkness, through a period of dark night. We are living in tragic times as we witness the process by which as a result of discoveries in the realm of physics, nature is deprived of its soul and devastated, and the cosmos, so to speak, made to disappear. Marx and historical materialism have deprived history of its soul and devastated it. Freud and psycho-analysis have done the same thing to the human soul itself. The end of the war and the revolution are revealing terrible cruelty; humanity is dim and fading out; the Creator is, as it were, withdrawing from His creation; He is present in it only *incognito* (a favourite expression of Kierkegaard). But all this can be understood as a dialectic moment in the revelation of the Spirit and the new spiritual life. One must die in order to come to life again. The crucifixion of man and of the world is taking place, but the last word will belong to Resurrection.

We are not yet entering into the era of the Spirit; we are entering into the dark era. There have been forerunners of the new revelation of the Spirit throughout the whole extent of the history of Christianity, and such there are also now. There are always spiritually-minded people who live before their time. The Eastern doctors of the Church were of great importance in their contribution to the interpretation of Christianity as the religion of the Spirit, especially Origen and St Gregory of Nyssa, the latter more than any other. His doctrine of man was the most exalted in the history of Christian thought, and his spirituality anticipates the whole history of Christian mysticism.[1] Further, the religious movement in Italy at the end of the twelfth and the beginning of the thirteenth centuries, which was a quest for the Christianity of the Holy Spirit, is of enormous importance.[2] Its central figures were St Francis of Assissi whose character most nearly approached to the pattern of the person of Christ, and Joachim of Floris who had prophetic premonitions, although sometimes they were naïvely expressed. In popular religious movements there was already something new. The apocalyptic frame of mind made its appearance in Europe after the French Revolution and the Napoleonic Wars, although it found very confused expression.[3] The German mystical movement which began in the fourteenth century and is represented by Eckhardt, Tauler and others, was of still greater importance for this change in consciousness. But Jacob Boehme and later Angelus Silesius were of greater significance than all.

German idealistic metaphysics of the beginning of the nineteenth century also constituted a most outstanding event in the history of the European spirit, in the dialectic of the divine and the human; and in spite of the mistaken nature of the monistic tendency in them they did prepare the way which led to the possibility of a new consciousness. German mysticism as a whole, however, inclines to be hostile to eschatological thought. It was in Russia that eschatological aspiration, with its expectation of a new epoch of the Spirit, and belief in the possibility of a crowning revelation, was most forcibly expressed. If we compare one of the greatest of Russian saints, Saint Seraphim of Sarov, with one of the most recent of Roman Catholic saints, Jean Baptiste Vianne, the Curé d'Ars, we are struck by the fact that in St Seraphim all

[1] See Jean Daniélou, *Platonisme et théologie mystique. Essai sur la doctrine spirituelle de St Grégoire de Nysse.*

[2] See E. Gebhart, *L'Italie mystique.*

[3] See Viatte, *Les sources occultes du Romantisme*, Vol. II.

his aspiration is directed exclusively towards the resurrection, towards the transfiguration of the whole creation in the Holy Spirit, that is to say, towards the future. In the Curé d'Ars everything is directed exclusively to the Cross, that is to say, to the past. The apocalyptic and eschatological trend is to be found also in popular religious movements in Russia and in the quest for truth by the Russian intelligentsia, as well as in the supreme moments of Russian religious thought. Here I ought again to mention names to which I have already many times referred, especially Dostoyevsky, Vladimir Solovëv and N. Fedorov, and even a man who stood apart from Orthodox thought, that seeker after truth, that seeker after God—Leo Tolstoy. The religious and philosophical movements which belong to the beginning of the twentieth century were coloured in the same way.

But quite one of the most notable of the forerunners of the religion of the Spirit was Cieszkowski, the philosopher of Polish messianism.[1] In him the conception of a religion of the Spirit as the crowning and complete revelation is expressed more clearly than in Solovëv. His thought passes outside the framework of historical Christianity, but it preserves a link with the Roman Catholic Church. The link with the Church is of great importance in this respect, that it saved the movement towards a new revelation of the Spirit from assuming a sectarian character. And this link becomes a possibility in the Orthodox Church in particular, for there are greater potentialities in Orthodoxy than in Roman Catholicism. In the Roman Catholic sphere Léon Bloy stands out as the great man of Apocalypse. There was a strong prophetic element in him. But in that stupendous writer, as indeed in many others, the prophetic premonitions were mingled with survivals of the old ideas of a sacrosanct monarchy, with the cult of Napoleon and the like. People like Kierkegaard have been of vast significance, but their influence acted indirectly. Charles

[1] See the book already referred to, Cieszkowski, *Notre Père*, in 4 volumes.

Péguy may also be considered as a forerunner of the era of the Spirit.[1]

But we must recognize as forerunners of the era of the spirit not only those who deliberately regard themselves as Christians, we must include also those who do not call themselves Christians and even those who are anti-Christian in their thought. The fact is that even the fight against God may be a way of serving God, it may be more truly religious than coldness and indifference. New ground is made ready by the tragic experience of man and the creative activity of man. Such forerunners of the era of the Holy Spirit cannot be called devout in the traditional sense. Nietzsche has enormous importance; his appearance was a highly significant moment in the dialectic of the divine and the human, without the consummation of which no new religious era can follow. Moreover, there is an important element of messianic consciousness in socialism too, for all that it is associated nowadays with atheism. Among the great writers of the end of the nineteenth century, Ibsen is to be noted as being of prophetic mentality; he used to speak of the Third Kingdom, the Kingdom of the Spirit. It is impossible to decide on rational grounds the position of the line which separates the Holy Spirit from Spirit, and that which is referred simply to Spirit may have a relation to the Holy Spirit, whose operation in the world is universal. God may not be where one would like to see Him, and He may be where one refuses to see Him. The presence of God in the world is mysterious, and not susceptible to precise definition. It is equally impossible to state precisely the boundaries of the Church. These limits are rigidly fixed only for the purpose of exercising power. Politics are the most fatal force in human life, it is they which have perverted the life of religion and stained the history of the Church with blood. The era of the Spirit will not tolerate the sway of politics over the life of the Spirit.

[1] In this connection there are rich materials in Romain Rolland, *Péguy*.

There was a very long period of human history in which consciousness was stabilized, and appeared to be immobile and unchangeable.[1] And corresponding to this stable consciousness was a certain condition of the world, which was regarded as the one reality. Belief, which is the unveiling of things invisible, was directed to a different world than the world which corresponds to the structure of average and normal human consciousness. The traditional spiritual philosophy of the schools, very abstract in character, recognized the spiritual nature of the human soul. But it opened up no new horizons upon other worlds than this, it has not stressed the possibilities of spiritual experience. Everything has gone on moving within established limits, within the order of the objectivization of Spirit, within the sphere of the antithesis of subject and object. But the objectivization of Spirit, its alienation from itself, its projection into the external, is the chief hindrance to a new out-pouring of the Holy Spirit in the world. The acknowledgment of objective Spirit which is indeed the objectivization of Spirit, is the greatest obstacle which the new spirituality, and the advent of the era of Spirit have to encounter.

Indian religious and philosophical thought has believed in the possibility of changing consciousness; in its view consciousness is dynamic. But any conception of the dynamism of history has been entirely lacking. In Christian Europe on the other hand there has been immense awareness of the dynamism of history, but the dynamic conception of consciousness has been lacking. Consciousness has taken a static form in the thought of Christian Europe, and with this has been connected the idea of the unchanging nature of man. The Indian conception of the dynamism of consciousness cannot satisfy us because of the monism of Indian thought and its failure to recognize the rôle of the human principle. It is in

[1] See my book, *Creativity and Objectivization*. An essay in eschatological metaphysics.

Christianity that this rôle is revealed.[1] The new era of the Spirit, the new consummating revelation will have as its counterpart a corresponding change in the structure of human consciousness. And this change in the structure of consciousness may be prepared for by spiritual effort. Objectivizations have corresponded with degrees of revelation. In the process of revelation, that which ought to be revealed from within and out of the depth, has appeared instead as something revealed from without and from above. Objectivization always means disruption and dichotomy; what Hegel calls the unhappy consciousness. The new revelation of the Holy Spirit brings alienation and objectivization to an end, not in thought only but in life itself, in vital spiritual experience; it is a movement in depth. Consciousness passes into super-consciousness and a world is revealed which lies beyond the sphere in which subject and object fall apart. This will mean a loosening movement of the indurated, petrified phenomenal world, and greater translucency in the noumenal core of the world.

Œcumenical religion is the religion of Spirit purified from enslaving elements; it is the religion of the Holy Spirit in whom is the fullness of revelation and all power of emancipation. And that is the eternal Gospel. Man is a mixture; there is in him a combination of creature and creator, he is compact of matter, absurdity and chaos, and yet he is the possessor of creative power to realize things that are new. Creativeness in the world is, as it were, the eighth day of creation. Really new life is created, not by the fact of man's setting before himself external aims in the realization of which he acquiesces in, and is even compelled to make use of, criminal means, but by this above all, that he radiates from within, from his own self, a gracious transfiguring creative energy. The new life, the new era of Spirit presupposes a total change in man and not merely a change in this or that separate part of him. It is a

[1] See the recently published book, O. Leombre, *L'Absolu selon le Vedanta. Les Notions de Brahman et de l'Atman dans les systèmes de Cankara et Romanoaja.*

moral, intellectual and aesthetic change, and at the same time a social change. And above all it is a manifest renewal of soul. There will be no special religious and ecclesiastical side of life but the whole of life will have become religious. It is only spiritually that man is an independent being. Biologically and socially he depends upon nature and society. That is why any social movement alone, unless a spiritual movement goes with it, is powerless, and may turn out to be merely the resumption of the old, though it wears new clothing.

Apocalypse depicts in symbolical form the destructive course of evil. But we must not interpret apocalypse as fate, as though the terrible results of the world process were inevitable. This would amount to a complete denial of freedom. It is only the path of evil which is fated. The path of good is constructed upon the freedom of man, who shares in the creation of the world. In the revelation of the Spirit, the apocalyptic end must appear in another light. The apocalypse of historical Christianity depicts the final destinies of mankind as a complete separation and breach between God and mankind, as being what Hegel called the 'unhappy consciousness'. The apocalypse of the religion of the Spirit depicts the final destinies of mankind as a divine-human creative act, as a work achieved by the collaboration of God and man. The positive end, the end which decides things, must depend upon man as well, not only upon God. Fate can be overcome by freedom.

The historical process divides into two, and its results may be appraised in two ways; but if there were nothing positive in its end the creation of the world would have been a failure. In the Book of the Revelation there is a prophecy of the thousand years' reign and the positive result of the world process is symbolized by this. But the historical Church has been much afraid of millenarianism and hushes it up. This symbolism must again reveal its meaning in a new way in the final revelation of the Spirit. The idea of the thousand years' reign has been left in historical Christianity in a lifeless and abstract state. It has been given life and made concrete in social movements which to all appearance lie outside Christianity. If the negative results of the universal historical process ought to be consumed in fire, its positive results must be thought of concretely, as a revived community life in all its fullness, as community inspired and maintained by freedom. If human life were to become the incarnate expression of a completely organized, mechanized and rationalized life of masses and not of peoples, if it were to become divided up into categories and at the same time completely totalitarian, that is to say if the last traces of freedom were to disappear, then spirit and spirituality also would disappear, for spirit is freedom. Free community can only be the result of a movement which is both spiritual and social, and in which the spiritual and the social cease to be separate and opposed.

The Incarnation and the earthly life of Jesus were an interpenetration of the two natures; the hand of God was laid upon the Chosen One. Only in the Resurrection was Jesus finally raised to infinite height. That which happened individually in the God-Man ought to happen in God-manhood, and that will be the third revelation of the Spirit. It is impossible to reconcile oneself to the idea that the creative vital impulse, the moments of luminous joy, of creative love and liberation, which have been experienced in ecstasy, will all disappear for ever, come to nothing and leave no trace. At the end of revelation there is infinity, not the sinister infinity which knows no end, but the good infinity which is eternity. There will be darkness and suffering in the future such as there have not yet been. But there will also be unprecedented light, there will be the appearance of a new man, of a new society, a new cosmos. There will be the crowning point of the mystical dialectic of the threefold being of God.

Pneumocentrism is already to be seen in the Gospel. Everything happens in the Spirit and through the Spirit. From a certain moment onwards this pneumocentrism will begin to increase. The Spirit has been stifled in historical Christianity and history has taken a line which is opposed to Christianity. This was the passage through the severance and rupture of the divine-human link. In the end it has been a death before the resurrection to a new life. A deadly anguish has gripped mankind, but the time will be shortened and the end of time will come. The Church which is beginning to convey the impression of powerlessness, of having lost the gift of the Spirit, will appear in its eternal nature, as inspired by the prophetic spirit. This is the Church as St John conceived it, the Church to which Orthodoxy makes the nearest approach. A Russian apocalyptic said that in Orthodoxy a great eschatological patience was to be found but in the deeps of it there was also great eschatological expectation. Into the Church of the Holy Spirit there will enter also everything creatively positive which has in appearance been outside the Church, and even been opposed to it. The eschatological problem is the final problem in the dialectic of the divine and the human.

CHAPTER XIV

The End of Things and the New Æon

The whole movement of thought in this book leads to the problem of the end, not as one out of a number of problems but as the all-embracing and principal problem. 'Thesis: The world has a beginning in time and it is confined within the limits of space.' 'Antithesis: The world has neither beginning in time nor bounds in space but is infinite, as in space, so also in time.'[1] This is one of the antinomies of pure reason in the transcendental dialectic of Kant's genius. What interests me here is simply the antinomy as it is associated with time, and it must be extended to include the apocalyptic problem of an end in time. The antinomies of Kant cannot be resolved, cannot be *aufgehoben*, to use Hegel's expression. Reason finds itself in the power of transcendental appearance (*Schein*). Kant is absolutely right in saying that the antinomies cannot be overcome within the limits of the phenomenal world. In the problem with which we are now concerned it is alike impossible to think that the world will exist endlessly in time, and to think that it will come to an end in time. For Kant there is no development which has its source in antitheses. Hegel's dialectic is quite different in character. With him the antinomies find their solution in dialectic development. Thesis and antithesis overcome each other and are removed in a synthesis.

Contradictions do give rise to development. The discovery of becoming, of development was an important discovery of Hegel's. The unity of being and nonentity gives rise to becoming, to

[1] Kant, *Kritik der reinen Vernunft. Antinomie der reinen Vernunft. Erster Widerstreit der transcendentalen Ideen.*

development. Development in the world presupposes nonentity. But with Hegel there is no end, nor any eschatology in the true sense of the word. The dialectic of the finite and the infinite is continually resolved, but never consummated. That is why it was possible for him to accept even so scandalous an end as that which made the Prussian State into an absolute monarchy. The two European philosophers of the greatest genius, Kant and Hegel, provide no solution to the dialectic of contradictions, for they have no doctrine of the end of things. This is provided only by prophetic religious experience, and that was outside the purview of both of them. There was partial truth both in Kant and in Hegel and they help one to comprehend the philosophical problem of the end of the world and of history, a problem which had hitherto been expressed in religious phraseology only.[1] It is not true to say that Hegel's dialectic is simply a matter of logic. It follows from his recognition of the identity of thought and being that the logical dialectic becomes a dialectic of being. It might be said, using the terminology of some of the movements in philosophical thought at the present time, that in Hegel there was an existential dialectic.[2] His theory of master and slave, and of the unhappy consciousness are of that kind.

We do not acknowledge the identity of being and thought; for us, therefore, the dialectic is different in character, and is connected with religious spiritual experience. There is a paradox in the fact that when there is no envisagement of an end everything becomes finite. Eternity is revealed only in the prospect of an end. The dialectic of antinomies is not resolved within the confines of our world æon, which bears all over it the impress of objectivization. Here Kant is more right than Hegel. But Hegel was more right than Kant in his recognition of development

[1] See my book, *Creativeness and Objectivization.*

[2] Wahl has interpreted him in this way; and so has Netty Nadler. See her book, *Der dialektische Widerspruch in Hegels Philosophie und das Paradox des Christentums.*

through contradiction, although the development does not arrive at any solution. There is a paradox in thinking of the end of time, the end of history, as occurring actually within this time. This is what makes the interpretation of the Apocalypse so difficult. One cannot think of the end of history either as happening within the limits of our vitiated time, as an event which belongs to this world, or as taking place outside historical time, as an event which belongs to the next world. The end is the conquest of both cosmic time and historical time. There will be no more time. This is not an end in time but an end of time. But existential time, which has its roots in eternity, remains, and it is in existential time that the end of things takes place. This will be the entrance into a new æon. This is not yet eternity, which men still try to objectivize. The sharp line which marks the frontier between the here and the beyond will be obliterated.

But there is a further aspect of the paradox of time. It lies in the fact that a mysterious coincidence of past and future is possible, a coincidence of origins and end. The eschatological problem is the fundamental metaphysical problem. Philosophers have given very little attention to it, almost none at all, because they have separated philosophical cognition from religious experience. And this is a false separation, it is a wrong interpretation of the antinomies of cognition. The world ought to end and history ought to end; otherwise everything is devoid of meaning. The end is the triumph of meaning. It is the union of the divine and human, and the eschatological consummation of the existential dialectic of the divine and the human. We ought to move forward, and it may be that we are already moving forward, into the time of the end, which will be of infinite continuance.

From the philosophical point of view the end of the world and history is above all the triumph over objectivization, that is to say triumph over the world of alienation, necessity, impersonality, and hostility. It is the formation of a world of objects which is the source of all the misfortunes of man. The object is alien and intolerable to me.[1] Hegel too connected the unhappy consciousness with relation to the object, with dichotomy and disruption. Consciousness is always dichotomy and disruption; it presupposes an opposition between subject and object that always involves unhappiness. The overcoming of dichotomy and objectivization, the way of escape from slavery to the world, to objects, may be called the awakening of super-consciousness or of the higher consciousness. Objectivization is always a cooling of the creative fire. In history there is a cooling development. It is what Péguy called 'politics' as distinct from 'mysticism'. The fate of monasteries, revolutions, communist colonies, Tolstoyans, Dukhobors, the fate of love ('only the morning of love is good'), the posthumous fate of men of genius, all tell of chilling objectivization. It is impossible to expect the final solution of world history along this line. Classical culture would seek to petrify the world, to fix it in rigid forms, whereas the world ought in fact to be fused and molten in the fire. 'I am come to send fire on the earth; and what will I, if it be already kindled?' These words have been forgotten in objectivized, cooled, Christianity. Man is crushed between two sinister infinities, and being in that position, desires so to order himself that he may not feel its tragedy.

The endless expanse of alien space filled Pascal with terror, but the endlessness of time in past and future is just as frightening. This double sinister infinity expresses itself in an existence which is projected into the external, that is to say in objectivized existence which is ever more and more disrupted from its noumenal core. In his discontent with the present man turns either to the memory

[1] Sartre, whose philosophy is fashionable nowadays, a gifted man, and very characteristic of our time, is in fact the slave of objectivity, the world of things, the world of phenomena, which has no reality in itself. It is a profound truth that reality depends upon the creative activity of man. But Sartre would think that behind the apparent there is nothing, there is no mystery. See his book, *L'Être et le Néant*, and mine, *Solitude and Society*.

of a golden age in the past or to the expectation of a golden age in the future. Man is capable of imagining a better, and fairer, a more truthful and just life than this unpleasing life. But whence does he get power for such imagining? Nor in any case will this power of imagination that he possesses vanquish the power of time, that fateful power of time, which holds sway even in his very conception of the golden age. Man materializes the thousand years' reign. The prophetic idea of the thousand years' reign is foreign to St Augustine. In his view the thousand years' reign was already realized in the historical Church. This left him in the power of objectivization. But historical Christianity is coming to an end in its fated way, and the inevitable transition to eschatological Christianity is taking place. Rays of light shine from the future. The final future unites with the sources of the past. There are three stages of revelation; revelation in nature, revelation in history, and eschatological revelation. It is only in this last that God finally and fully reveals Himself. This stage is preceded by a state of Godforsakenness, by yearning anguish, by the mechanization and devastation of nature, by the mechanization and secularization of history, and by transition through a period of godlessness.

Eschatological revelation is also revelation in Spirit and in Truth, which is eternal revelation. There is a tragic clash between Truth and the world. Pure undistorted Truth burns up the world. The goal is the attainment of wholeness, the overcoming of disruption, the surmounting of false antinomies in thoughts, dreams, passions, emotions, desires. There may be suffering in the dissevered parts of the soul, whereas in other parts of it there may not be. It is only because suffering does not grip the whole soul that man can exist, but his existence is unhappy. Universal history recalls to the mind not only tragedy but comedy also, and comedy always comes to an end in the same way. It is the fatal failure of history about which I have already spoken. All efforts to create a new life, whether in historical Christianity, by social revolutions, or by the formation of sects and so forth, alike end in objectivization, and adaptation to dull, everyday normality. The old rises in new forms, the old inequality, love of power, luxury, schisms and the rest. Life in our æon is only a testing and a pathway, but the testing has a meaning and the path leads to a consummating end. It would become easier for man if he were aware of the fact that a further revelation of the unknown is at hand, a revelation not only of the Holy Spirit but of a new man and a new cosmos.

A passive and an active eschatology are both possible. In the majority of cases the apocalyptic frame of mind has led to a passive waiting for the end, and a refusal to face the problems of history. Such was *The Story of Antichrist* by Vladimir Solovëv. Apocalyptic time is interpretated as a time of mere waiting for, and submitting to, the action of divine and diabolic powers. This is a decadent temper of mind. But an active eschatology is possible; and that imposes a knowledge of self which answers to the dignity of man as free spirit. It asserts the need to strengthen human activity and human creativeness when the end comes. The thought of the end must be grasped not in a passive and negative attitude of mind but creatively and positively. I have already said that every creative act of man is eschatological in character and brings this world to an end. The end is interpreted in different ways according to whether man looks at it from the point of view of historical Christianity, or from that of the more complete revelation of the Spirit. In the latter case man is a subject not an object, and he is a creative subject. Christian consciousness has reflected too little upon the fact that the race of mankind will come to an end if all men become completely Christian, absolutely continent, or monks. Here the eschatological depth of the problem of sex comes into view. It is commonly said that the end of marriage is the begetting of children and that that is the supreme good. But at the same time it is thought that this supreme good is the result of what is considered vicious and sinful. Rosanov exposes very acutely and vigorously the hypocrisy which results from this inconsistency. Solovëv and Kierkegaard alone thought that in the actual begetting of children there is something vicious and sinful.

The metaphysics of sex has an immediate connection with the problem of the end. When the end comes something will be changed in the life of sex. After the submergence of this side of life in horrifying darkness and dissolution enlightenment must come. Love can transfigure the old sexual life and direct the energy of sex which holds man in bondage, into creative channels. We are aware of the possibility of such sublimation of energy. Love will be given a central position in the religion of the Spirit, the religion of the end, love which is creative and transfiguring. Both eros-love and agape-love will play such a part. But before entering upon the higher epoch and reaching unity man will have to follow to the end the path of dichotomy and the way of suffering which is scarcely to be borne. It must always be remembered that at the end of His path Jesus cried, 'My God, My God, why hast Thou forsaken Me?' There was a man who at the end of a long historical path also experienced abandonment, Godforsakenness, of another sort, and that was Nietzsche. The world process is tragic in character; it cannot be understood as a continuous progressive movement forward, The evil results of the world process, for all that they may even increase, are thrown out into non-being, but men and women, living creatures, cannot be finally cast into non-being. There is only one thing which perhaps earns the eternal pains of hell and that is the too insistent defence of them, accompanied by a feeling of satisfaction.

The greatest religious and moral truth to which man must grow, is that we cannot be saved individually. My salvation presupposes the salvation of others also, the salvation of my neighbour, it presupposes universal salvation, the salvation of the whole world, the transfiguration of the world. The very idea of salvation arises from the oppressed condition of man; and it is associated with a forensic conception of Christianity. This ought to be replaced by the idea of creative transformation and enlightenment, by the idea of perfecting all life. 'Behold I make all things new.' It is not only God Who makes all things new, it is man too. The period of the end is not only a period of destruction, but also a period of divine-human creativeness, a new life and a new world. The Church of the New Testament was a symbolic image of the eternal Church of the Spirit. In the Church of the Spirit the eternal Gospel will be read. When we draw near to the eternal Kingdom of the Spirit the torturing contradictions of life will be overcome and sufferings which towards the end will be increased, will pass into their antithesis, into joy. And this will be the case not only for the future but also for the past, for there will be a reversal of time and all living things will share in the end.

Principal Works by Nicolas Berdyaev

DATES given are those of the original publication in Russian or French. The symbols E., F., G. signify respectively the existence of English, French or German translations and, where the titles differ from the Russian, these are given.

1900. 'F. A. Lange and the Critical Philosophy.'

1901. 'Subjectivism and Individualism in Social Philosophy.'

1907. 'Sub Specie Aeternitatis.' 'The New Religious Consciousness and Society.'

1910. 'The Spiritual Crisis of the Intelligentsia.'

1911. 'Philosophy of Freedom.'

1912. 'A. S. Khomiakov.'

1915. 'The Soul of Russia.'

1916. 'The Meaning of Creativeness.' (G. Der Sinn des Schaffens).
'The Fate of Russia.'

1923. 'The Meaning of History.' (E.)
'Philosophy of Inequality.'
'The World-Outlook of Dostoievsky.' (E. Dostoievsky).

1924. 'The Russian Religious Idea' in 'Problems of Russian Religious Consciousness' 1924. (F. 'L'idée religieuse russe' in Cahiers de la Nouvelle Journée No. 8).
'The New Middle Ages.' (E. 'The End of Our Time' which includes four other essays).

1926. 'Leontiev.' (E.)
'Philosophy of the Free Spirit.' (E. 'Freedom and the Spirit.')

1931. 'The Destiny of Man.' (E.)
'On Suicide.'
'Russian Religious Psychology and Communist Atheism.' (E. 'The Russian Revolution.')

1931. 'Christianity and Class War.' (E.)
1932. 'Christianity and Human Action.'
1933. 'Man and the Machine.' (E., including other essays, in 'The Bourgeois Mind.')
1934. ' "I" and the World of Objects.' (E. 'Solitude and Society.')
'The Fate of Man in the Modern World.'
1937. 'Spirit and Reality.' (E.)
'The Origin of Russian Communism.' Only in French and English.
1940. 'Slavery and Freedom.' (Of Man.) (E.)
1946. 'The Russian Idea.' (E.)
1947. 'The Existential Dialectics of the Divine and Human.' French (E. 'The Divine and the Human.')
1949. 'Towards a New Epoch.' (E.)